Dear Bruce and Masami -

Thank you for serving as role models and as inspiration for those couples who dream of working together.

Frank and Sharon

November, 1988

WORKING TOGETHER

WORKING TOGETHER

Entrepreneurial Couples

FRANK&SHARAN BARNETT

Ten Speed Press

The Barnetts welcome comments and questions about
this book, Working Together Seminars and workshops,
and the National Association of Entrepreneurial Couples (NAEC).
Write to Frank and Sharan Barnett
National Association of Entrepreneurial Couples
Box 825, Belmont, California 94002
or call (415) 594-4800
FAX (415) 595-4331

Ten Speed Press
P.O. Box 7123
Berkeley, California 94707

Book and Cover Design by Barnett/Associates, Aptos, California
Typesetting by Metro Typography, Santa Cruz, California
Text set in Sabon on the Mergenthaler Linotron 202

Library of Congress Cataloging-in-Publication Data

Barnett, Frank, 1939–
Working together.

1. Couple-owned business enterprises—United States—
Management. 2. Work and family—United States.
3. Interpersonal relations. 4. Businessmen—United
States—Interviews. I. Barnett, Sharan, 1947– II. Title.
HD62.27.B37 1988 658.4'09 88-24829

ISBN 0-89815-276-3
ISBN 0-89815-266-6 (pbk.)

First Edition
Printed in the United States of America

1 2 3 4 5—92 91 90 89 88 cloth
1 2 3 4 5—92 91 90 89 88 paper

Dedication

We dedicate this book to that strange and wonderful entity that seems to reside somewhere between every entrepreneurial couple. It is not *him*, it is not *her*, and it is much more than *them*. We have referred to it variously throughout *Working Together* as *synergism*, *Our Brain* and the *Three Hundred Percent Think Tank*. We're not quite sure how it lives or functions, but we are eternally grateful for its existence.

Contents

Foreword

Nearly fifty years of working together has proven at least one thing with absolute finality—small is better. So we are delighted to see the publication of a book which, in terms of practical advice and examples of case histories, celebrates the "old-fashioned" idea that the family business as a basic method of functioning is not only sensible but at least as efficient as the big business concept of corporate constellations.

Not that a family business cannot get to be big—as indeed, several examples in this book can testify—but rather there are enterprises in which only the small approach can work successfully. Couples have launched businesses that might not have existed had it not been for the special power of cross support which two individuals totally committed give to each other and their enterprise. A partnership that supplies action photos for rodeos and another that does specialized cross-continental trucking are just a couple of the happy surprises in *Working Together.*

A firm which has grown into being on the strength of a relationship as close as that of husband and wife can never get to be impersonal. Impersonality—basically, not really giving a damn about what it is you are doing—is the root of inefficiency, and worse, of boredom. Whereas the firm that your partnership has created, the business you have argued over, fought for together, worried about and worked at for outrageous hours, becomes a mutual triumph. You share an emotional investment which, willy-nilly, acts as a cement to further strengthen your personal relationship as partners, and makes you far more aware of the personal relationships among the people you employ. In a word, you *care*.

When we talk about having worked together throughout our married life, people tend to look bemused, if not downright incredulous. And only half-jokingly they ask, "*How* have you done it?" There is this idiotic myth that husband and wife cannot, indeed perhaps should not, work together, as though working would threaten their personal relationship.

The truth is, we probably could not have succeeded in either endeavor—marriage or work—without the support of the other activity. Each of us is a strong-minded individual with a need to concentrate interest with function. Had our career objectives been widely divergent, we would probably have had to go our separate ways since neither of us would have had the time for, or interest in, the activities of the other.

The profession we entered together (the first American branch of Penguin Books, consisting of ourselves and a stock-boy) was publishing, which eventually, when we started our own firm, allowed for the expression of a wide latitude of personal interests and aptitudes.

Our early experience had forced each of us to learn all the roles in publishing—editing, accounting, marketing, promotion, art, production, packing, shipping, switchboard, warehousing, whatever—not all with equal skill, of course, but sufficiently well so that from time to time, when the chips were down and there happened to be too few of them each of us was able to function in any area of the business, acting as a double, or sometimes, triple-chip. And most of the people who worked with us were the same way, because when you are small, you learn to make every stroke count. Things were never, ever, dull.

Whatever interests we were pursuing or expressing in book form (and these included the environment, history, the future, science fact and science fiction, music, the west, sex, politics, dogs, literature, war and other manifestations of the human condition) it was all done on a very personal basis; the welfare and destiny of each book was a matter of intense emotional interest and the health and purpose of the business was a passionate concern.

Banal as it may sound, this is what life is all about. This is why we enjoyed working with a group of dedicated spirits, and why, we believe, they were dedicated in the first place. (Incidentally, there were three other sets of married partners working at Ballantine Books besides ourselves.) The partnership approach was, and is, one helluva lot of fun. It was also heartache and depression, and triumph and high elation. This is why we admire working couples and would not have wanted it any other way for ourselves, and still don't. Somewhere in the mutual gut, we share the feeling that the world would be better off if more couples found a way to work together.

Which brings us directly back to the fascinating subject of this book. In the thorough exploration Frank and Sharan Barnett have made in *Working Together*, they highlight and detail the many reasons why and how a couple can succeed in running an enterprise. Nowadays, a number of new factors have come into play that increase the chances of success for a new business. The computer, for instance, is vital in easing the problem of overheads and makes the home-run enterprise far more viable than it used to be. But still more potent are the ideas in *Working Together* as they clearly demonstrate that a couple is greater than the sum of its parts. Small is not only better, it is much bigger than it knows. We sincerely hope that this book will help you to make that truth an exciting reality.

Bearsville, New York   Ian & Betty Ballantine
September 1988

Acknowledgments

We would like to thank all those very special people who helped to make this book possible, many of whom have played pivotal roles in our lives over the years and others of whom we came to know as we researched and wrote *Working Together*. A loving thanks to our children, Anthony, Elliott, and Kimberly, who from the very beginning of our copreneurial venture served as sounding boards and critics, accommodated our deadlines, and, most important, cheered us on.

Although our parents live hundreds of miles away, they too played important roles in our project. Frank's mother, Kay Barnett, was always available by phone—even at the most ungodly hours—to listen, encourage, and offer cogent suggestions. Sharan's parents, Ken and Corinne Sturdevant, contributed the invaluable suggestion that we contact Mayflower Transit, Inc.

We appreciate the enthusiasm that so many expressed for our project and their assistance in referring entrepreneurial couples. In particular we would like to thank Eric Anders, traffic manager at Mayflower, who gave so generously of his time and knowledge so that we could tell the Mayflower story and meet copreneurs David and Nancy Laffen; and Rick and Sue Ramirez, who learned of our project over dinner one evening and referred us to Rick's brother Peter de Haydu and his wife Marina of Christine Valmy, Inc.

Our partner, Donna Loevenich, provided encouragement from the very first day, when the three of us sat together over lunch and discussed our idea for this book. Without her assistance in discovering couples who work together and her willingness to hold down the fort during our investigative travels, this book would have taken much, much longer to write.

We are particularly grateful to George Young, editor-in-chief, and Philip Wood, publisher, of Ten Speed Press, who had faith in our abilities and the foresight to recognize the significance of copreneuring as a new social movement. And we are deeply indebted, and just a bit awed, by Jessie Wood's uncanny ability to become part of *Our Brain* during the copy editing of *Working Together*.

Finally, to our many new friends, the copreneurs who appear in this book, we acknowledge your participation with the realization that *Working Together* is really *your* story. The synergism that we all shared during this project is characteristic of the spirit of copreneuring. Thank you all for your willingness to serve as role models and to share your thoughts and pioneering experiences with your fellow copreneurs and those couples who wish to gain positive control of their work and personal lives.

Aptos, California   Frank & Sharan Barnett
August 1988

A Note
to Our Readers

As you read this book, you will quickly discover that we often refer to ourselves in the third person. In our writing, we have found this to be the most natural way to deal with the fact that we are both *actors* in the story of *Working Together* as well as the *storytellers*. Writing about ourselves was tricky because of the collective "we" and the individual Frank and Sharan.

Our writing process is a collaboration. While other writing teams may divide their work and write separately, we sit side by side at the same computer, sharing the keyboard and screen, writing together. Once we have completed a writing project, it is impossible for us to unravel our work to determine which of us wrote this or that sentence, or to whom a particular thought might be attributed. As we write and create, we bounce ideas off each other, often completing one another's thoughts. To the consternation of our friends, this joint thought process carries over into our conversational style, with one of us often finishing the other's sentence.

Gradually we have come to realize that it is not just Frank and

Sharan who are involved in our daily creative process, but that the synergism between us has resulted in what we affectionately refer to as "Our Brain." Ideas that result from our collaborations can really not be identified as either Frank's or Sharan's, and therefore we laughingly consider them to be the creation of Our Brain—something we share between us, but which does not exist without both of us.

Not long ago we were sitting in a restaurant, just before we were to interview another couple for *Working Together*, and Sharan remarked, "How am I doing? Am I contributing enough to the book? I feel like I just sit down at the computer and follow you along." Frank's reply was, "Are you kidding? That's exactly what I've been feeling!" We were silent for a moment and then Sharan asked, "Well, if I'm not writing this book, and you're not writing this book, then who the hell is?" The answer to that question is, quite simply, we *all* did—my brain, your brain, and Our Brain!

Preface

The inspiration for *Working Together* did not strike us like a bolt from the blue; rather, it was the culmination of a process spanning several years. During that time we worked together, lived apart, lived together, worked at separate jobs, and gradually found ourselves growing closer, both in our personal lives and in the worlds in which we worked. The result of our experiences led to this book. *Working Together* draws not only on our own personal experiences but on the experiences of other entrepreneurial couples as well.

Today, there are many books dealing with alternative work and life choices. Unfortunately, far too many of these "how-to" books have been authored by fast-track professionals seeking personal recognition and validation. When all is said and done, their successes can only be duplicated by readers who possess a rare constellation of similar talents, skills, training, education, and background. Far too few of us are able to apply these authors' messages to our own lives. Unlike those self-help books, *Working Together* has broad applicability. If you are contemplating becoming an entrepreneurial couple, you'll find real life examples of how other couples—real people just like yourselves—became successful coentrepreneurs.

Now more than ever before we need answers that can be realistically put to work. Our daily newspapers highlight troubled economic times—a staggering foreign debt, a huge trade imbalance, low productivity, and falling living standards. We are bombarded with sobering news of the demise of the middle class and the continuing obituary of the work force—layoffs, shut downs, mergers, and buyouts. While the gap between the very rich and the very poor widens, those of us in the middle find ourselves stymied by the sustained stillness of our economic growth. Working together as an entrepreneurial couple, or *copreneuring*, is one response we can make toward taking control in an economic world turned upside down.

In these pages we will dispel the myths of working together, address the social biases, look at the benefits and risks and outline the steps you can take toward a successful shared work and life experience. This book was written for those who are exploring the notion of working together, as well as those who are already entrepreneurial couples. We can all gain insight into our relationships and share a sense of community with the couples we meet in this book.

At the conclusion of our study we were left with a picture of healthy personal relationships as well as successful and creative enterprises. However, during the course of our investigation pitfalls and problems did emerge, and have been included in our frank discussion of entrepreneurial couples. Thus *Working Together* is not only a celebration, it is also an objective examination of the positive and negative aspects of copreneuring.

In embarking on the research for our book, we were careful not to approach the subject of entrepreneurial couples with preconceived notions or biases, taking caution from Albert Einstein's observation, "It is the theory which describes what we can observe." Operating on the belief that the interview process itself would supply the answers to questions we quite possibly did not even know at the outset, we worked without any operating hypotheses or assumptions. Our methodology was to interview couples already working together, and to let them tell their stories, in their own words, allowing their experiences to reveal the truths about copreneuring.

Our approach was not to impose ourselves and our experiences on the material but rather to let our findings speak to us, providing revelations and new insights. Our sole criterion was to select only those entrepreneurial couples who were in twenty-four-hour-a-day business and personal partnerships, and whose business relationships were *outwardly equal*.

In the past few years many authors have focused their spotlights on "celebrity" couples in business together. We recognize that such "superstars" as Elisabeth Claiborne Ortenberg and her husband Arthur, who founded Liz Claiborne, Inc. in 1976, and Debbi and Randy Fields, who established Mrs. Fields Cookies, Inc. the following year, are inspiring models. However, we have opted to seek out couples whose stories have not yet become part of the folklore of successful copreneurs. Many of the couples interviewed for *Working Together* founded and operate nationally recognized businesses, and while they are not today's celebrities, they may indeed become tomorrow's superstars.

Initially we discovered our couples by poring over books and newspaper and magazine articles that dealt with the subject of entrepreneurs. Within that broader category we ferreted out companies headed by entrepreneurial couples. Many of our leads were just snippets—sometimes only a line or two, a brief mention here or there.

Few of our reference sources dealt head-on with the subject of copreneuring. And those that did more often than not were written in a style that trivialized the subject or diminished the very real business enterprises under discussion. Many writers found it difficult to approach copreneuring free of stereotypes and without merging the often unrelated topics of romance and love with the equally serious issue of being in business.

Much of the material we reviewed emphasized the lighter and less important aspects of the partnership. Specifically, these articles highlighted the angle of Mom and Pop, or love and romance in the workplace, even when dealing with large and successful corporations. Some titles sounded more like *Modern Romance* than *Forbes*—"Labors of Love," "Honey, What Do You

Say We Start Our Own Company?," "Becoming Partners in Work and Love," and "In Love and Business: The New Partnerships," while other titles reflected a prevalent cultural bias—"Ma 'n Pa in Big Deals."

These views of couples working together are deeply rooted in the American workplace. Many corporations adopted anti-nepotism policies during the fifties and sixties to avoid the employment of incompetent relatives. Such policies have been broadly expanded to exclude the employment of spouses within the same organization. And many companies demand that if a couple meet on the job, one of them must find other employment.

A report published in 1988 by the Bureau of National Affairs suggests a need for corporations to reevaluate those policies. It appears that the negative consequences of couples working together are often the result of the negative perceptions and jealousies of co-workers. In fact, many companies today are discovering that couples working in the same organization can be a real asset—when both partners have a stake in the company's success, loyalties can be twice as strong.

A recent focus on love in the office has brought a flurry of articles in mainstream news publications and television news segments across the country. Unfortunately, this attention has not brought about a new realization that as employees couples can often bring higher levels of communication, as well as shared goals and commitments, to company objectives. Not only have the negative aspects of couples working in a company been advanced, but a recent California Fair Employment and Housing Commission ruling has given employers greater leeway to refuse to hire husbands and wives. This ruling sets a new standard for judging marital discrimination claims and sets the equal rights of married couples in the workplace back more than thirty years. All of this has contributed to biases and to a preoccupation with love in working relationships when entrepreneurial couples are placed under scrutiny.

Balance sheets are subject to quantification. Love and romance, while very real emotions, are purely subjective. Clearly, many of the copreneurs in this book are deeply in love and more than a few, after decades of marriage, have managed to keep the spark of romance alive. However, from the outset the central focus of *Working Together* has been the entrepreneurial relationship, not the aspect of love or romance.

This is not to suggest, however, that love and romance do not play a significant role in copreneuring. On the contrary, we feel that the power of love and romantic passion can be the catalyst and fuel for many entrepreneurial couples. Dr. Ethel Spector Person's study, *Dreams of Love and Fateful Encounters: the Power of Romantic Passion* (W. W. Norton & Company, 1988) a brilliant exploration of our concepts of love, observes that love in the twentieth century has been ignored as a subject worthy of scientific observation. This omission has its roots in the propensity of science to deal only with that which can be explained.

In examining those characteristics common to the entrepreneur—in particular, the ability to embrace risk and accept change and growth—we've discovered, in Dr. Person's study, parallels between the entrepreneurial personality and the liberation of self brought about by the experience of love. In her central thesis, Dr. Person argues that "Romantic love offers not just the excitement of the moment but the possibility for dramatic change in the self. It is, in fact, an agent of change."

> Love creates a situation in which the self is exposed to new risks and enlarged possibilities; it is one of the most significant crucibles for growth. Romantic love takes on meaning and provides a subjective sense of liberation only insofar as it creates a flexibility in personality that allows a break-through of internal psychological barriers and taboos, and sometimes external ones as well. It creates a flux in personality, the possibility for change, and the impetus to begin new phases of life and undertake new endeavors.

Over and over again, all across the country, we encountered couples whose enterprises exemplify just such endeavors. The leaps of faith and affirmations of trust we discovered can only be explained by the deep love and commitment that many of these couples bring to both their relationships and their enterprises.

Our interviews of copreneurs for *Working Together* began close to our home in Aptos, California, a village on Monterey Bay. Gradually, as couples and associates became excited about our project, they began to suggest other copreneurs throughout the country. The owners of a French bakery in Capitola, California insisted that we contact a couple in Providence, Rhode Island who own and operate two gourmet restaurants. Our local bookstore suggested a husband-and-wife team in Santa Barbara, California who write and illustrate exquisite children's books. Husband-and-wife designers in Phoenix, Arizona said we "just had to meet" the couple who had founded a creative cookie company in Tempe. And a tip from an investment advisor in Aptos led us to a meeting in New York City with his brother and sister-in-law who own a nationally renowned cosmetics firm.

Phone call after phone call to copreneurs across the continent elicited an overwhelmingly positive response to our project, leading finally to a marathon of interviews from coast to coast. Eventually those interviews took us through twenty-one states and the District of Columbia. The stories of twenty-four of those couples, in addition to our own account of what it means to work together, appear throughout the pages of this book—fifty individual copreneurial tales in all.

Early on, we decided not to use questionnaires to gather information. We felt that only face-to-face meetings in each couple's place of business—offices, factories, stores, studios, clinics, restaurants, salons, farms, stables, and homes—would yield the true picture of today's entrepreneurial couples.

We elected to interview couples together, rather than to schedule separate meetings with each partner. This process allowed us to watch the copreneurs in action, and much was revealed by their interactions, body language, and facial expressions as they pondered questions, occasionally disagreed, and often laughed together during their meetings with us. One respondent, unsuccessfully trying to help his partner find just the right word to express her thoughts, turned to her and quipped, "I'm *supposed* to be able to read your mind!"

All of the couples examined here are quite special, and their backgrounds and enterprises are varied. We met with couples of all races, a variety of religious beliefs, and diverse educational backgrounds. Their vocations range from truck drivers to authors, cowboys to manufacturers. We interviewed copreneurs of all ages, the length of whose personal relationships ranged from just a few years to nearly four decades. Their stories have been woven throughout the fabric of our text to illustrate and highlight the variety of ways in which these copreneurs have dealt with issues of shared work and life experiences. These exciting and creative couples are, in a very real sense, today's economic pioneers.

Until quite recently couples in enterprises together were rarely viewed as equal partners. The image of Mom and Pop was applied to even the largest of ventures and, more often than not, coentrepreneurial enterprises were viewed as businesses in which males were the "makers and shakers" and their wives the "helpful little troopers." As a result of these stereotypes we felt a new term was needed to describe the egalitarian entrepreneurial relationships that exist in growing numbers in today's business community.

Cultures have always been mirrored in their language and English is no exception. In today's rapidly changing society, new words are added daily to the arsenal of our language. Ralph Waldo Emerson observed, "Language is a city, to the building of which every human being brought a stone." And the stone we are contributing is *copreneur*—not just a shortened version of "coentrepreneur"—but a new term charged with meaning and a sense of vision for a new kind of partnership. Copreneuring is based on trust, equality, sharing, and intimacy between partners. It involves not only a commitment to a particular enterprise; it reflects a life style that incorporates the work and personal worlds. Throughout this book the terms *copreneuring*, *coentrepreneuring*, and even what we refer to as *the new Mom and Pop* are used interchangeably, reflecting this new spirit of equally shared entrepreneurism.

Today, many circumstances are contributing to a social and economic climate that allows entrepreneurial couples to be accepted in their professions as viable economic entities. These factors have been brought about by the social and cultural changes that have taken place since World War II.

During the late forties and fifties, the generation that had experienced the hardships of the depression and the war sought the security of working for someone else, preferably a large company. In the 1960s, those Americans born during the war had little interest in entrepreneurial enterprises, focusing instead on issues of social justice. By the mid-1970s, however, entrepreneurship was becoming an attractive alternative to working in America's sluggish and declining industries.

In the sixties, only a few universities offered courses dealing with entrepreneurship. Less than two decades later, nearly three hundred and fifty institutions of higher learning included such courses, with at least half a dozen offering majors in the subject. At Harvard, fifty percent of the students enroll in courses focusing on entrepreneurship. The pendulum has swung away from the view that once favored large corporations. A 1988 Roper poll reported that only seventeen percent of Americans now hold large corporations in high regard, and that ninety-one percent define the American Dream as the opportunity to start their own business.

The women's movement has played a pivotal role in the rise of entrepreneurship as well. Never before in history have so many women worked; nor, for that matter, been expected to work. Entrepreneurship has been an avenue for women seeking to achieve the promises of the feminist movement. In fact, women have been joining the ranks of the self-employed at a rate three times faster than total self-employment growth, and the Small Business Administration estimates that by 1999 there will be as many businesses owned by women as by men.

We cannot overlook the importance of the personal computer, which has made it possible for a small privately owned and operated business to compete with the largest corporations. Now, in the late 1980s, we are seeing an explosion in the establishment of home offices. Telecommunications and personal computers aside, the creation of home offices and entrepreneurial enterprises is in part a reflection of America's desire for the security of strong personal ties and a dissatisfaction with the old ways of working, which separate and uproot us

geographically and psychologically from our family and community. Throughout our meetings and discussions with entrepreneurial couples, we were impressed with the emphasis that
they placed on traditional family values.

Increasingly the fortunes of large companies are falling, while
small businesses continue to add new vitality to the American
economy. According to the U.S. Bureau of Labor Statistics,
almost eleven million American workers found themselves
looking for new jobs following company cutbacks and plant
shutdowns between 1981 and 1986. As a result of this decade's
buying, selling, restructuring, and downsizing of corporate
America, the stigma of being fired has all but disappeared.

Over one and a half million jobs with Fortune 500 companies
evaporated between 1974 and 1984, a period during which there
was actually a net increase of twenty million new jobs. Of those
new jobs, three-fifths were created by small independent
businesses.

It could be said of today's economy that there are two Amer-
icas, one composed of large corporations, the other of small but
vital businesses. These fourteen million small enterprises are
fueling the engines of a new economic era. Each year, another
one and a half million entrepreneurs join those forces. While
small firms may have a higher frequency of failure, the job
security they have provided during the 1980s has over all been
equal to job security in larger businesses.

The American dream of becoming your own boss has been
rekindled; today that dream is being realized by almost ten
percent of the American work force. Just how many of those
entrepreneurs are, in fact, couples working together cannot be
determined from the statistics presently available. However, it is
worth noting that data from Internal Revenue Service-based
information reveals that one of the fastest-growing categories of
tax returns is that filed by Joint Owned Non-Farm Sole Proprietorships. According to the Small Business Administration,
most of these enterprises are run by couples who live together.
This classification of returns grew at an annual rate of 10.2
percent during the period 1977 through 1983, while all non-
farm sole proprietorships grew at an annual rate of 5.8 percent.

In 1977 there were 257,899 jointly owned non-farm sole

proprietorship tax returns out of a total 8,413,406 filed with the IRS—3.1 percent of all returns. By 1985, 3.6 percent of all returns, 482,933 out of 13,296,751 filed, were businesses in this classification—an increase of almost a quarter of a million businesses in less than a decade. Another factor that further obscures the number of couples working together is the still prevalent practice of husbands who list themselves as the owners of businesses in which their wives participate on a full-time basis.

Even with the small amount of extrapolation that might be possible from the IRS-based data, it is impossible to obtain a true picture of the invisible force that copreneurial couples are exerting on the economy today. No statistics are available on partnerships or corporations headed by couples, and seventy percent of the couples we interviewed work together within a corporate structure.

Statistics aside, when you examine your own immediate business community you will discover just how prevalent copreneuring has become. From retailers to manufacturers, from restaurateurs to fashion designers, from franchisers to video producers—they are everywhere, and their ranks are growing. And these copreneurs are not only showing us a new way of doing business and acting as role models; they are blazing new paths for all of us in the realm of personal relationships as well.

PART ONE

Becoming
A Copreneur

OTAM

For far too many of us, employment controls our lives, uprooting us from our communities and isolating us from family and friends. Copreneuring is one way to regain positive control of our lives and become personally responsible for our futures.

CHAPTER

1

An End to Separate Lives and Separate Agendas

There was a time when couples and families worked together, assuring the well-being of their small economic units. There was a time when communities banded together, providing their members with social and political cohesiveness. And there was a time when work was not only linked directly to survival, but also contributed more to personal satisfaction and sense of self.

This book is about a return to a way of life which, until the development of the industrial age, had served mankind well. And it is about a particular group of pioneers, today's copreneurs—entrepreneurial couples who are showing us one way in which we can regain the values of that gentler time.

These copreneurs are drawing upon a basic economic unit that is older and more solid than any economic system now in existence. Their ventures are based upon the firm foundation of the family unit as an economic enterprise, in which the couple's individual energy, experience, vision, and sense of purpose are combined into a partnership based on trust, equality, sharing, and intimacy. They utilize interdependency and open communi-

3

cation between equal partners—ingredients that are rarely found in outside employment settings. These exciting couples have developed a modern version of an age-old economic unit, and are showing us a way to return to independence and the security of self-reliance.

Our society has come to accept that our work quite naturally assumes control of our lives, uprooting us from the communities in which we live and isolating us from our families and friends. For far too many of us, our lives are out of our own control. We find ourselves in employment that brings us little personal satisfaction, autonomy, or joy.

In exchange for what we do in the workplace, and for the personal sacrifices that work demands, we are compensated monetarily for both our productivity and our losses. To make up for the sense of emptiness that arises from the separation of our personal and work lives, our conditioned response has been to fill the void with material goods. But those personal sacrifices have been too great, and the price we have paid through the diminishment of our lives too high. Mere material goods are a sorely inadequate substitute for the bonds of human contact that many of us have lost.

The copreneurs you will meet in this book have regained control of their work worlds as well as of their personal lives. In many ways, these couples have successfully blended those two realms, the work and the personal, into a harmonious whole. *Working Together* is a celebration of a group of individuals who are showing us one path out of an economic way of life that undermines many of our most basic psychological and emotional needs.

Everyone, young or old, will find inspiration in the stories these couples tell of themselves and their enterprises. The oldest business we encountered, which has been thriving for nearly two decades, was established when its founders were in their early twenties. And the dean of our copreneurs, who will celebrate his seventieth birthday as this book goes to press, established his business with his partner fifteen years ago, when he was fifty-five. The youngest business you will meet is a dynamic and profitable start-up, less than a year old, which is expected to gross five million dollars in its first twelve months.

You will encounter businesses that still operate out of homes —and that's exactly how some partners want it, having planned it that way from the beginning. Other ventures that began at home, on kitchen tables, in living rooms, garages, and barns, have grown well beyond those early days, now occupying imposing facilities and employing large staffs. In fact, over half of the twenty-five businesses you will meet originated in the founders' homes.

In nearly three-fourths of the couples we interviewed for *Working Together*, at least one of the partners had made a career change to begin their new enterprise. And in well over half of these ventures, both partners committed to a career change that enabled them to work together.

Whether you are toying with the notion or giving serious thought to working together, the couples in this book will provide inspirational role models, illustrating that there are powerful options to working alone in a competitive world. You will see that these couples have not allowed any obstacles, however seemingly insurmountable, to keep them from persevering toward their goals. The synergism that takes place between two intimate partners can be truly dynamic. It is astounding what a single human being can accomplish alone, but these adventurous couples have proven over and over again that two can accomplish far more together than the sum of both working separately.

When we began our search for copreneurs, we didn't know who or what we would find. At the end of our interviews, back in our office, having traveled thousands of miles crisscrossing the country, we began the process of organizing our materials. As we do with so many of our creative projects, we hung large sheets of paper on the walls around us. Each sheet carried a different bit of the data gathered during our journey. On one we wrote the names of all the copreneurs we had interviewed. A second sheet listed their geographic locations, and others broke out information regarding lengths of relationships, ages of

couples, number of children, categories of businesses, how long
each business had been operating—anything that might provoke
thought and contribute to the brainstorming and organization
of this book.

We found that these couples had nothing in common with
one another, beyond the fact that their relationships extended
into both their personal and business lives, and that they shared
a mutual commitment to excellence in the products or services
they provided. Many of these couples worked by themselves,
some had small staffs, and others had large numbers of employees. They were in the country, they were in the city, they
worked out of their homes, shops, offices, factories, in every
conceivable work setting. They sold books, drove trucks, hauled
horses, manufactured cosmetics, baked cookies, carved decoys,
produced videos, held auctions—and each and every one of
them loved what they were doing and wouldn't trade places
with anyone else in the world.

Most important, these are people who are in control of their
lives, doing work they love, and doing it together. Time after
time, we heard, "I have to pinch myself every now and then just
to make sure it's real. I'm doing exactly what I've always wanted
to do, and I'm making a living at it. And I'm doing it with the
one person in the world I care most about."

Not only are these copreneurs earning a living at what they
enjoy, they are passionately committed to making their businesses the very best that they can be. They are producing the
kind of products or providing the services they themselves
would demand of others, recognizing the unquenchable thirst
for quality among today's consumers. It didn't take us long to
realize that if it's excellence you're seeking, your search will end
at the doorsteps of businesses run by entrepreneurial couples.
We soon came to anticipate this, and as we traveled from
business to business, in state after state, we were never
disappointed.

These enterprises are run by individuals who create their own
methods, design their own equipment, and even invent their
own products. And if they are producing an already existing
product, they make it unique and better, putting their own

stamp of excellence on it. The copreneurs we met are not content with the status quo—they continue to improve their businesses and products, massaging and refining, always remembering that there is room for improvement. As one copreneur told us, "The good have to be desperately better." And almost every couple we met confided that they would never work as hard as they do for anyone else.

A business can be a very demanding mistress; if either partner in the businesses we explored had established and maintained their enterprise as an entrepreneur rather than as copreneurs, their personal lives would have been greatly affected. Many entrepreneurs whose spouses are not involved in their business acknowledge that the pressures of their enterprise, along with the extraordinarily long hours required to launch and run a successful business, can place strains upon personal relationships that often escalate to the breaking point.

Copreneurs are entrepreneurs who never need to go home and explain to an uninvolved spouse what's going on at work. The inevitable late hours, setbacks, and losses as well as the discoveries, triumphs, and growth are all understood and shared equally between these partners. Moreover, these copreneurs brainstorm and discuss problems and opportunities spontaneously, receiving instant feedback. The spontaneity with which these couples operate allows their businesses to change and respond to market needs quickly and efficiently.

Many of the businesses we visited were ventures that had experienced periods of phenomenal growth, bearing out what one copreneur told us. "When there are two of you, anything can be accomplished." To copreneurs, obstacles become opportunities; tell copreneurs "It can't be done," and they'll find a way to prove you wrong.

In spite of the time and energy copreneurs invest in their businesses, they are individuals who have come to the realization that they are successful not only because of their own hard work, but also because of the support of their customers and their communities. These couples can be found addressing business and community groups, organizing cultural events, committing time and enthusiasm to their local schools, churches, and synagogues, and lending their support and talents to local, regional, and national fund-raising events and charitable organizations.

The owners of a bookstore learned first-hand the importance of the interplay between the community and their business. When they relocated their store to larger quarters, their customers voluntarily organized a moving party, providing refreshments and manpower, making what could have been an exhausting ordeal more like an old-fashioned barn raising—a community celebration of *their* book store and a joyful event. As the owners stated, "Everything we give, we get back."

We met copreneurs who relate to their business very much as if it were a part of the family, recognizing that it has needs and demands that must be met and balanced, almost like a child. However, these businesses were not started as family firms, and for the most part must be distinguished from family enterprises that were established with succession as an objective.

While family members often participate in these copreneurial enterprises, their participation is not a result of the expectation of the founders. And yet, because of the freedom that the partners have to define their own work environment, their children can often be found in the workplace. We encountered babies in offices, an eight-year-old grandson who performs *real* work in his grandparents' store, a brilliant young craftsman working with his parents in their studio, and children who were surprised to discover that the homes of their friends did not have computers, editing studios, or rooms bustling with employees. And we met adult children of copreneurs who are actively involved in management positions in their parents' companies.

Very few of these enterprises were undertaken with the primary objective of getting rich or making a fast buck. The formation of these businesses represents a commitment to a lifestyle in which the relationship between the partners is an integral part of the whole, and in which personal security is not necessarily defined by the wealth those businesses can generate. In fact, some copreneurs pointed out to us that if they were to compute their earnings on an hourly basis, the net result would jingle rather than crinkle—they would be earning less than minimum wage. It isn't the money that drives most copreneurs on—it's the independence they feel as a couple, the power of self-reliance, the total commitment and involvement in a service or product over which they have absolute control, and the gratification they receive from working together.

In a partnership based upon trust, there is no need to prove oneself right or the other wrong. Individual egos merge into "wegos"—a combined ego, shared noncompetitively by the partners and directed constructively outside the relationship.

If we began our investigation with any bias, it was on the issue of *Mom and Pop*. In our own business we worked hard to maintain a professional image by down-playing our personal relationship. For us, the image of Mom and Pop was of the corner grocery store, with Dad behind the counter and Mom at the register—not at all the sophisticated and creative image we wanted to project. Mention Mom and Pop to us in the context of our own business and our hackles would rise.

However, through our interviews with other copreneurs we came to a new appreciation of that concept. A new Mom and Pop have come on the scene today, running both large and small enterprises. And we discovered that some copreneurs *insist* on viewing themselves and their businesses as Mom and Pop enterprises, courting and even capitalizing upon that image.

Seeking an explanation of why some couples wish to view themselves as Mom and Pop and others don't, we discovered a concept that divides products and services into "warm" and "cold" categories. These new Mom and Pop enterprises all deliver a product or service that can be classified as "warm;" that is, one in which the human or emotional element plays a primary role, and in which the partners are often, although not necessarily, involved directly with their clients and customers. Thus a veterinarian whose business is caring for pets—emotional units within the family—is providing a "warm" service, while the products and services of our advertising agency are clearly "cold," since we have no personal contact with the ultimate consumer of our creations, the public.

We would fall into a trap if we assumed that copreneurial

businesses can be classified as "Mom and Pop" based simply on the criteria of size or dollar volume. We encountered new Mom and Pop enterprises whose businesses and incomes far exceed the wildest dreams of any corner grocery store; some of these Moms and Pops head multimillion-dollar operations. Conversely, other copreneurs who head relatively small operations do so in a style and with products and services that cannot in any way be viewed as a Mom and Pop enterprise.

Whether or not a couple considered themselves to be a Mom and Pop organization, all of the copreneurial enterprises we encountered exhibited a high degree of communication, trust, shared objectives, and freedom from interpersonal competition between the partners—attributes that are in short supply in many other business environments in this country.

As the stability of big business and corporate America dwindles, many couples are retreating to the high ground of an older and more proven institution—the family unit. And the core of the family has always been two individuals committed to a deep personal relationship and to the common good of that economic unit.

A copreneurial enterprise tests the personal relationship and the strengths of each partner. It is an opportunity for couples to produce their own economic resources in today's uncertain times. Not only do these couples grow and mature within their enterprises, but—perhaps of even greater significance—they bond together within their personal relationships at a speed and in ways that never would have been possible without the experience of working together.

During one of our interviews, we received this cogent observation on the social and personal implications of working together.

> In the long run, we're sharing the burden equally; and no matter how tough it is to put your head on the pillow at night because you're worried, the other person putting their head on the pillow next to you is equally worried, or equally proud, or equally elated. Our relationship has matured much faster because we've worked together.
>
> Working together is a great way for people to have relationships

—and it's a great way for people to be entrepreneurial. I'd recommend it to everyone. Copreneuring is the future.

The self-made man has always been a cultural ideal. Today, the self-made couple is a personal response to a changing economic and social climate. The copreneurs in *Working Together* are a true cross-section of the pioneers in a rapidly growing social and economic movement in America.

If we were to paint a picture of the average couple in this book, the woman would be in her early forties and her partner would be in his midforties. Their maturing enterprise would have passed through that critical first five-year phase characterized as "start-up," and be approaching the celebration of its tenth anniversary.

Statistically entrepreneurs start businesses during their early to midthirties. Therefore, our average copreneurs are members of the first wave of pioneering couples who can be studied, providing the first relevant data from which conclusions can be drawn concerning the phenomenon of copreneuring. Our average copreneurs have reached maturity—and so have their enterprises. These forty-year-olds can tell the world's thirty-year-olds what to expect.

The spirit of the entrepreneurial wave of the eighties is swiftly being transformed into the copreneurial wave of the nineties. During the coming decade, copreneurial enterprises will emerge in ever-increasing numbers. With the conviction that all the indicators point to a rapid rise in copreneurialism, we have written *Working Together* as a guide for couples who wish to stop the old way of life apart and begin a new supportive life together as copreneurs.

To be an entrepreneurial couple is to become personally responsible for your collective future, to let go of the "security" of two pay checks, to discover who both of you really are and take positive control of your lives. Once you realize the benefits and joys of copreneuring, working alone will never again seem a viable alternative. Working together is an end to separate lives and separate agendas.

CHAPTER

2
Begin with
Your Best Friend

Clients and strangers alike often find it hard to believe that a husband and wife can work together intensely, day in and day out, remaining friends and functioning as individual professionals in the competitive business world. Some are incredulous, others genuinely interested, perhaps questioning their own isolated personal and working relationships. Most simply accept that couples spend little time together, and that's the way it has to be. When the subject of working together is brought up, usually prompted by curiosity, we've learned that our responses invariably elicit tales of how couples have structured their lives to create distance, rather than togetherness, between themselves and their mates.

More often than not we hear, "I couldn't do it. It would drive me crazy!" At a client's Christmas reception, the wife of one of the vice presidents could hardly contain herself when she discovered we were a husband-and-wife creative team. "How do the two of you stand it? My husband would drive me nuts! We could never, never work together." Not long ago, a friend jokingly commented, "If my wife worked with me, I'd shoot her

13

in the head by noon." And we have often heard, "What am I going to do when my husband retires? He'll be home all the time!"

Jim, who operates a small sailboat dealership out of his home, arranges to spend most of his time at the harbor, sometimes with customers, more often just puttering around aboard a boat, to keep out from under his wife's feet. "The house is Donna's job," Jim often says.

> If I hang around, she'll think I don't have anything to do and slap a paintbrush in my hand. Besides, if we were together all the time it wouldn't be as much fun. This way, we're glad to see each other when I come back home.

Hugh, a marketing executive, marvels at our ability not only to work together, but also to enjoy each other's company on a twenty-four hour basis. Hugh and his wife, Linda, whose names have been changed here to protect their privacy, have been married for nearly thirty years and during that time have built a relationship grounded on structured separateness. Linda doesn't work outside their home; Hugh is always the first to arrive at and the last to leave his office. At home their distance continues with little or no discussion of Hugh's daily achievements or setbacks. Hugh's work is a world so far apart from his wife's daily activities that many of his colleagues have never even met Linda. In a recent conversation, Hugh observed,

> Fortunately, Linda values her independence as much as I do. We couldn't survive without our separate rooms to retreat to. Once we bought a large two-bedroom condominium. There was no den for me and no extra room for Linda. It didn't take long for us to discover that we needed three bedrooms—one apiece and one to share. In the end it just didn't work. We had to find a bigger place.

Hugh and Linda clearly have a strong relationship and commitment to one another. Their separateness is not a reflection of any lack of affection or love, but it does mirror the cultural times during which their relationship was forming.

During their early years together, in the fifties and sixties, their unconscious acquiescence to the rules of corporate America and accepted role stereotypes resulted in a style of relating that works best in isolation with brief times of real togetherness. Hugh and Linda's interaction is an extreme example of engineered separateness, the opposite end of the togetherness continuum. Still, their story is more comprehensible to most than is the vision of a totally egalitarian coentrepreneurial experience.

TESTING THE WATERS

The fascination expressed by so many toward our partnership prompted us to examine our own personal and working lives together. We knew that we had discovered, almost from the beginning, a collective strength far beyond our individual capabilities. In a society based on independence—even within personal relationships—our choice had been to merge all aspects of our lives.

As copreneurs, hardly a day goes by when one of us does not look up to be struck by the realization that the person sitting behind the other desk is a spouse as well as a partner in the corporation. Our partnership has become an alliance that stretches from corporate board rooms to our bedroom.

Our decision to work together as partners evolved as a process. We were fortunate to have been best friends before deciding to form our own company. One of our principle assets was having had the opportunity to test the waters by working together for other firms before striking out on our own as copreneurs.

We met at work; and although we initially did not work together, those early months provided opportunities to observe each other's capabilities, working styles, and ethics. Much later, when we were no longer working for the same employer, we found ourselves collaborating on Frank's projects. Frank was working for a publisher, negotiating contracts, editing books, producing newsletters, and directing photo sessions, and Sharan found herself increasingly drawn into his work.

We would sit at the breakfast table editing Frank's manuscripts or writing catalog copy. When photo sessions were scheduled, Sharan found it impossible not to become creatively involved. She would make suggestions for content, and occasionally the two of us would actually set the shot up the evening before or rise early in the morning so Sharan could participate and still be on time to her job.

The creative aspects of publishing appealed to Sharan to such a degree that when a position opened as Frank's assistant, the two of us successfully lobbied for her employment. Securing that position for Sharan was quite a feat in itself. Frank's employer had begun his company in partnership with his wife. Unhappily, their relationship had ended in a bitter divorce. As result, when we first broached the subject of Sharan's possible employment, days of discussion ensued and we learned that he felt that working together was not healthy for a marriage. In addition, he argued, "If one of you becomes dissatisfied and leaves, I'll probably lose both of you."

Nevertheless, Sharan got the job, and for the first time we were actually working together, sitting side by side, writing at the same computer, sharing the same keyboard. We quickly discovered that we enjoyed working together, and our most significant revelation was that collectively we were much more creative and productive than when working apart!

Sam and Libby Edelman are another couple who had the benefit of being able to test the waters before creating their own enterprise. In December of 1987 the couple entered the contemporary footwear market as Sam & Libby, California. They began with a clear purpose—to wakeup the industry with a line of shoes and boots that would provide fresh and innovative designs at affordable prices.

After their first nine months of operation, this start-up company had shipped to every state in the country, and their shoes could be found in virtually every important department store from Bloomingdale's to Robinson's, Macy's to Nordstroms—they've all shown their support through large orders. Sam boasts, "There's no major store that we haven't shipped our goods to with the name Sam & Libby on them."

In a miraculously short time the couple has shown three

formal collections. In fact, Libby comments, "We realized we had designed enough shoes to support a fifty million dollar company." In spite of the corporation's brief history, Sam and Libby feel confident enough to project that they'll be around for the next fifty years. Already, their back orders total three and a half million dollars. And they've developed a strong banking relationship that allows them the borrowing power their young company requires.

Their success is no accident. Sam and Libby are recognized leaders in the shoe industry with a proven track record in design, product development, and marketing. With a combined work background that includes such top shoe companies as Esprit, Kenneth Cole, and Calvin Klein, and major fashion magazines such as *Harper's Bazaar*, *Mademoiselle*, and *Seventeen*, the Edelmans possess a unique ability to accurately identify trends in the contemporary shoe market.

When the couple met in New York, Libby was the footwear fashion editor for *Seventeen* and Sam was working with his father, who owned Lighthouse Footwear. Four years after their marriage, the Edelmans were presented with a rare opportunity to work together at Esprit in San Francisco, where at thirty-one Sam became president of Esprit's shoe division and Libby, who was just approaching her third decade, assumed the position of merchandise manager of footwear and national sales manager for Esprit Kids Shoes.

Together they brought sales of Esprit shoes from zero to fifty-five million dollars, at wholesale, in only four years. This phenomenal growth can be attributed to the many highly successful shoe concepts and designs developed by the Edelmans. The couple's finely tuned sense of timing brought to the marketplace the "woven huarache" shoe, the "sweater boot," and the "silver penny loafer"—all fashion sensations. As Sam recalls,

> Esprit was a wonderful opportunity for us both. We tested the waters big time. We thought a lot about not working together, about the negatives, but there were many husband-and-wife teams at Esprit, and Libby and I made the commitment to join them. And that decision was the right one. It was a good testing ground for us. Our personal success and exposure there were phenomenal and our remuneration was very good for a young couple.

However, during those years at Esprit their individual responsibilities were made even more separate by the paranoia that couples often experience when working together as employees of the same organization. Although there are situations where working closely together can accomplish more, such intense interactions are often viewed by outsiders as an unnecessary self-indulgence. In fact, we had that experience when we were employed by the same publisher. Sam recalls how he and Libby went out of their way to avoid the appearance of abusing the system.

> We thought if we traveled together to Brazil people would say, "Oh, they're going to Rio to go to the beach, not to the factory." There is a level of paranoia that comes from working as a couple for other people, versus the positive force that results from working as a couple for yourselves.
>
> When we were at Esprit, I think Libby should have gone to Brazil with me. And believe me, I didn't go to Rio de Janeiro, I spent all my time in a small, unattractive, industrialized city, staying in a tiny hotel room that made Motel 6 look like the Plaza. But Libby never went with me because there could be somebody who would see two tickets and ask, "Why are they going together?" When really, the attitude should have been that perhaps by working together we might have accomplished even more.

In their own business the Edelmans often travel together. In addition to their corporate headquarters in San Carlos, California, which employs fifteen people, Sam and Libby have established a design studio in Parabiago, Italy; a fashion office in France; and a production office in Brazil where a staff of forty oversees the manufacturing of their fashion shoes. By traveling together and sharing responsibilities, which they weren't always able to do at Esprit, Libby has learned to understand the world-wide approach and all the different aspects of design and marketing that Sam & Libby, California has undertaken.

Sam and Libby have discovered that it is much easier to work together as coentrepreneurs than it was to work together as coemployees. At Esprit, because they didn't hold equal titles, Sam was not able to share information totally with his wife.

Today, in their own organization, they share equally the burden of building and managing a complex international organization. But in spite of their positive cash flow and high visibility in their industry, Sam insists that he would trade everything he has in the world for the experience he gained in their first nine months of operation. "What I've learned from our enterprise about our relationship is as enriching and as important as any financial gains we might get from it."

When asked about the image of their new company, Sam admits with pride that the fashion concepts of Sam & Libby, California have been built around the image of his wife.

> I think Libby has the greatest personal style of almost anybody in the fashion business. At Sam & Libby we're using Libby's style and personal point of view as the motivation of our organization. I really admire Libby, and the term "best friends" is too light for what we feel for each other. I think we have to come up with a new word. Libby and I have more belief and more loyalty for each other than just best friends, and that's what keeps us going.

FROM FRIENDSHIPS TO PARTNERSHIPS

Many of the couples we interviewed either met at work or created opportunities to work together before striking out on their own. One such couple is Ian and Betsy Weinschel, who for the past nineteen years have worked together as media consultants. Their firm, River Bank, Inc., is a state-of-the-art studio located on their picturesque one hundred and fifty acre farm in Mt. Airy, Maryland, an hour's drive from Washington, D.C.

The Weinschels have gained national recognition for their involvement in nearly seventy political campaigns. Their work has been used by an impressive list which includes President Gerald Ford, Vice President George Bush, Senator Bob Dole, Senator Charles Percy, Senator Bill Roth, and the 1984 Reagan/ Bush campaign. All of us have seen and been influenced by their exquisitely crafted political television commercials.

Ian and Betsy's business evolved out of their friendship, and they established their working collaboration before forming

River Bank, Inc. Ian recalls how their working relationship began.

> I was editing commercials and Betsy would come in at night. Looking over my shoulder, she would ask, "Can you move that shot around?" I wanted to show her what I could do and I would say, "Sure I can!" I'd move things around and then look at it for a while and decide I liked it better with Betsy's changes.
>
> We continued working like that, informally, during the evenings. Betsy kept coming in and I began to lean on her. Eventually it got to the point where I'd ask, "What should we change?" "What can we do with this?" "Is there anything we need to do before I show it in the morning?" It was kind of like Rumplestiltskin spinning straw into gold—we'd work at night and have our collaborative product ready to go in the morning.
>
> Early on, I learned the benefit of the sharing process when I was creating. It made everything a lot stronger and I didn't want to lose that relationship because no matter how well I could structure something, Betsy could come in and make it better.

The success of Betsy and Ian's working and personal relationship is the result of the strong bond that has grown between them over nearly two decades. Occasionally business will demand that one or the other must travel alone. Betsy laments,

> It's so difficult when Ian is on the road. Some people like to have quiet time by themselves, but I'm lonely when Ian is gone. It's like part of me is missing. And if anything is going to go wrong, that's when it will happen.

Ian values his friendship with Betsy and their working partnership.

> The basis of our relationship is that we are best friends. That's the most important thing. I liked being with my best friend, so we found ways of extending our friendship. If you are going to work, why not build a business around the things you like? Life seemed to be very short and was going by, so we built a business around the things that we liked with each other.

Although River Bank, Inc. is highly successful, it is their friendship that is primary, not the business. Betsy underscores this, emphasizing,

> If the business disappeared tomorrow, we would do something else together. We raise cows and all our own food. As long as our place didn't evaporate we would be perfectly content to sit there and not go out. I'm not sure we could work independently. I guess we could adjust, but I can't think of not working together.

After reflecting on Betsy's comment, Ian underscored his commitment to their friendship.

> We would *have* to work together. It's nice that we are media consultants and that we're successful, but the important aspect of our success is our friendship and our feeling of self-sufficiency. Those factors contribute to our creativity. We can do what we want, take more risks and express ourselves.

Johanne Killeen and her husband George Germon, both self-taught chefs, have worked together since 1975. Inspiration for their first venture, Al Forno, a trattoria in Providence, Rhode Island, resulted from living and traveling throughout Italy. For a time, Johanne worked in a tiny restaurant outside Florence, and George taught for the Rhode Island School of Design's European Honors Program in Rome.

Their first restaurant catapulted the couple to the forefront of young American restaurateurs. Today they own and operate a nightclub in addition to their two nationally acclaimed restaurants, Al Forno and Lucky's. Recently, food writer and critic John F. Mariani placed Johanne among the top twenty women chefs in the country, and in June of 1988 *Food & Wine Magazine* placed George and Johanne among the Ten Best New Chefs in America at the Aspen/Snowmass Food and Wine Classic, a three-day event attended by more than a thousand people from around the country.

Meeting with the couple at Lucky's, overlooking the Providence River in a renovated nineteenth-century stable, we dis-

cussed their relationship. The level of friendship between
George and Johanne is evident in their warm interactions, and
in their statements of deep commitment. Mirroring Betsy
Weinschel's comments, Johanne expressed her appreciation for
living and working with George.

> I love working with George. The times that we are separated, even
> for a couple of hours, are just not as much fun. I love the inter-
> change that goes on between us and think it's a very important part
> of why we are where we are, and what we've accomplished. I think
> it's a tremendous thing. We're definitely best friends.

From couple to couple, friendship emerged as the central
theme in their working relationships and seemed to go hand in
hand with their successes. In contrast to George and Johanne or
Ian and Betsy, Bruce and Masami Handloff's personal and
professional relationship is very new. They work together building their chiropractic and massage therapy practice, Handloff
Chiropractic, in Santa Cruz, California. Bruce is a chiropractor
and Masami is a shiatsu massage therapist. Like most copreneurs, they began as best friends. Bruce recalls, "From the first
time we met we just stuck together like glue. We became great
friends before anything else."

As a foreign student with an expiring student visa, Masami
was facing a return to Japan. Backpacking in Yosemite, she and
Bruce discussed their future. The realization that time was
running out forced the issue of marriage. As Bruce looks back,
"We were best friends then and I didn't want to lose Masami.
So, I figured the only way not to give up my best friend was to
marry her and not have to think about life without her."

Today Bruce and Masami are partners in a growing practice
that includes a registered nurse who is a certified acupuncturist
as well as a second massage therapist. They are still learning to
bridge the cultural differences between their very different
backgrounds—Bruce's relaxed California lifestyle and Masami's
traditional Japanese upbringing. Bruce reflects,

> Our references are different. Because of where we came from,
> things have different meanings. Being a woman and being a man is
> a big difference. But add to that the distinctions between Japanese

and American cultures, and the net result is a tremendous difference in the way our minds work. And yet we are a perfect complement to each other and work well together.

David and Suzanne Brown faced a dilemma similar to that of
Bruce and Masami. The story of how they met and married is a
poignant tale of lifelong friendship.

The Browns own and operate Plantation Farm Camp, Inc., a
working farm and summer camp not far from Mendocino,
California, where they met as eight-year-old campers over thirty
years ago. Plantation, which is in its fourth decade of operation,
is steeped in tradition, and David and Suzanne have been a part
of that lore since childhood. Their relationship evolved from
campers to counselors to caretakers and finally to owners of a
business that today includes a summer camp, a working farm,
and management of a redwood timber forest.

Before purchasing Plantation in 1984, David and Suzanne
lived in Fort Collins, Colorado, where both were educators.
Today they live at Plantation with their three children and
manage the farm's five hundred and forty acres and three hundred and sixty animals, as well as the summer camp's one
hundred and sixty campers and thirty-six employees.

Plantation has played an important role in the development of
many young people, but to David and Suzanne the farm has
been a central focus of their lives since childhood. After graduation from college they were presented with the opportunity to
live for a year at Plantation as caretakers. The culmination of
that year's working partnership was their marriage ceremony at
lakeside on the picturesque farm.

David and Suzanne's marriage occurred at a major turning
point in their lives. As a conscientious objector, David was
leaving Plantation for alternative service. Eleven days before
his departure, he pondered his impending separation from
Suzanne. "I literally didn't want to lose my best friend. In the
course of the year living here at Plantation, we had become very
close and it just seemed to me that marrying my best friend was
a very logical thing to do."

Even though the copreneurs we interviewed come from di-

verse backgrounds and are engaged in vastly different enterprises, we were struck by the similarity of their responses when
the issue of friendship came into the discussion. It was uncanny
to hear the same response—often the same words—in so many
different voices. Bruce's comments were echoed by David,
Betsy's by Johanne, and on and on it went.

THERE'S NO BETTER PARTNER

If you are considering breaking away from the traditional
world of work and starting a business, we recommend that you
consider doing so with the full support of a partner. And we
feel you can find no better partner than your *spouse, significant
other*, or however you define that special relationship—*your best
friend*. We make this recommendation with the knowledge that
copreneuring is not for every couple.

We discussed this with Susan and Barry Brooks, founders of
Cookies From Home, located in the heart of old town Tempe,
Arizona. In 1981 the couple brought Susan's family cookie
recipes to Tempe and opened a turn-of-the-century Victorian
cookie parlor. Today, their operation has expanded to include
direct mail, corporate sales, and, most recently, the distribution
of frozen cookie dough to over three hundred Arizona grocery
store freezer cases. Although Susan and Barry are passionately
committed to copreneuring, they too realize that it's not for
everyone. Susan contributed this insightful admonition.

> Many people think that if they have a good marriage, getting into
> business together would be a natural extension of that. And if they
> don't understand that working together is a very unique dance and
> not for everyone, it can cause trouble. It doesn't mean that the
> business is good if you *can* work together and it doesn't mean the
> relationship isn't good if you *can't*. Not everybody has that figured
> out.

Certainly, there are some couples who should not be working
together. You can look around and identify them quite easily.
More likely than not, *they'll* tell you they can't before you even

have a chance to ask. But perhaps the chemistry required to make a copreneurial relationship work is not as rare as we have been led to believe. After all, we don't need to look too far back into history to find a time when the family unit was an economic island—a time when families worked together, husbands, wives, and children.

We have all too easily come to accept the isolation that most of us experience daily, traveling to work alone, working independently of our colleagues, and returning home to a partner from whom we are separated for most of our waking lives. Today's two-income household is one in which both partners must reassimilate on a daily basis, in which each partner is removed from the other, and in which conscious and meaningful communication must regularly be reestablished.

In contrast to the isolation experienced by so many couples, the maturity and completeness of the relationships that characterize the copreneurs we met is really quite remarkable. These individuals appear to have added new layers of friendship, understanding, trust, acceptance, and maturity to their established relationships. Even in those rare instances when we encountered relationships that seemed to be fraying at the edges before the establishment of a copreneurial enterprise, we discovered to our surprise that as the couple's venture grew and became increasingly secure, so did their personal relationship.

Thus, although some experts might caution against entering into business together unless the relationship is absolutely in balance, we feel that couples should follow their intuition and the dictates of their own unique emotional chemistry. Often the things in our society that separate us from one another, compartmentalizing our lives, are the very things that are placing strains on our personal lives. We do not subscribe to the belief that absence makes the heart grow fonder, and look optimistically to the future and the couples of the 1990s who we predict will in increasing numbers choose to spend more time playing and working together.

In the businesses we examined, we discovered individuals who experienced growth at accelerated rates, far beyond what might be anticipated in other forms of relationships. We concluded from this that new metal most certainly results from the cauldron called a copreneurial enterprise. In any copreneurial endeavor there exists a fire that tempers those individuals who have the courage to enter into business together.

One explanation for the tremendous growth copreneurs can experience is that couples who go into business together already have a foundation based on friendship, communication, trust, and confidence—a foundation that expands as the couple proceeds together in their own venture. Where this foundation already exists, we believe that you can find no better person than your very best friend with whom you can immediately begin building a business together. When your partner is your best friend, someone you can trust, rely upon, and talk to, you will not be alone in creating and running your venture.

Independent entrepreneurs can find themselves virtually alone in their business. Unless they have a staff or outside consultants upon whom they can rely, they lack the sounding boards so necessary in any business enterprise. Thus they are forced to make even the smallest decisions in a vacuum. Most business failures are attributable not to a lack of capital or a ready market, but to a scarcity of time and personal resources at the disposal of a single owner. Sooner or later, these limitations can bring even the most promising enterprise to an impasse—and quite possibly to its knees.

When we established Barnett/Associates, a successful advertising agency that had its roots in our living room, it didn't occur to either of us to create a business plan that excluded the other. And today, with the benefit of hindsight and experience, we feel an even greater commitment to the concept of copreneuring.

By combining forces we have been able to capitalize on one another's strengths, share in the responsibility of decision making, and fill in the gaps for the other when required. As equal partners, we have the personal resources between us and the time necessary to address all the demands that our business places upon us. Our relationship, like those of all the copreneurs we met, is a harmonious blend of deep friendship and strong commitment to the passion that we daily invest in our creative endeavors.

CHAPTER

3

Getting on
the Right Track
Together

It is a curious phenomenon that much of our lives and most of our careers are determined by happenstance. Our education, more often than not, has little to do with our vocation. Randomness characterizes the course of most of our working and personal lives.

The average person will hold twelve different jobs in a lifetime, and three of those will call for career changes. Increasingly in today's workplace, a move is precipitated by forces outside our own career plans—economic slumps, mergers, and the downsizing or outright collapse of companies.

For an individual who is an entrepreneur at heart, the uncertainty of outside employment is even greater. At the core of the entrepreneurial spirit is the need for change and experimentation. When employed, the average entrepreneur is three times more likely to be fired. As a breed, entrepreneurs are an altogether different kind of animal. Their psychological profile characterizes them as high achievers who are driven and restless, taking fewer vacations than the average worker. When told "It can't be done," they swing into action and make it happen.

27

Entrepreneurs are Renaissance people who devise their own methods of working, often designing their own equipment and techniques to produce and market products that have never before existed in the marketplace.

Entrepreneurs are visionaries, capable of conceptualizing their enterprises before the first spadeful of dirt has been turned over, before the first brick has been laid, and before the company name is on the door. And the true entrepreneur has the vision to see the product or service that is already there, but that has eluded everyone else's attention.

Entrepreneurs are often characterized as risk takers, but they are not gamblers. They assess not only the feasibility of a project, but also their belief in their own ability to bring their dreams to reality. Entrepreneurs are committed to doing whatever is necessary to get the job done—no task is beneath them, no detail too small. The most significant trait of every entrepreneur is the conviction that they would rather work sixteen hours a day for themselves than eight hours a day for anyone else.

SOME OF US JUST AREN'T MEANT
TO BE EMPLOYEES

As Frank approaches his fiftieth year and looks back at the patchwork quilt of his career, the entrepreneurial threads are evident even before his graduation from high school. In his senior year he founded a summer day camp, and before his nineteenth birthday was heading an operation that had leased a swimming school, purchased a school bus, enrolled fifty children in the first season, and employed a staff of nine counselors. Too young to drive his own bus, he hired a driver; because of his age, the only insurance coverage he could obtain for his business was through Lloyds of London.

Within a few years, Frank successfully negotiated the sale of his camp to a larger operation and was off to run his own printing brokerage in Los Angeles. In addition to a graduate degree in anthropology and a brief stint as a college instructor, Frank has had a successful career in publishing as well as having founded and operated a bookstore, two fine-art galleries, and an advertising agency.

Frank has been self-employed for most of his adult life. During most of those brief periods that he spent working for someone else, he views himself as having been *misemployed*. Occasionally, however, fortune would shine on him and he would land in what he refers to as an "employment oasis"—one of those rare work havens where employers are mentors and growth is an important ingredient in the work formula. To Frank, the consummate entrepreneur, the rest of his employment was a vast wasteland. Fortunately, he can count those years spent in misemployment on the fingers of one hand, with a few left over to thumb his nose irreverently at those brief and unpleasant employment situations.

When Frank received a telephone call from an old friend informing him of a publishing position about to be vacated, it was totally unexpected. Frank's call to the publisher resulted in an interview the next day in a distant city. After less than half an hour talking across the publisher's desk and a forty-five minute lunch, he was offered the position of publications director. Sharan's successful interview with the same employer a month later lasted a brief thirty minutes. For both of us, life-altering decisions had to be made quickly and could be based only on intuition and the pressures of our economic realities.

In no other area of our lives are we expected to react so quickly and with so little information and advance planning as when applying for and accepting employment. We enter into other relationships much more cautiously. Very few of us would consider marriage based only on a short interview and conversation over a Caesar salad! And yet our work lives consume at least as much, if not more, of our time and energy as do most of our personal relationships.

As the result of a single unexpected phone call, Frank found himself in a new position, the two of us met, and together we embarked on a relationship that would ultimately lead to our own copreneurial experience and this book.

After our marriage, we moved our newly blended family,

Sharan's daughter Kimberly and Frank's sons, Anthony and Elliott, to a new city and worked for separate companies for a time, Frank for another publishing firm and Sharan as a legal secretary. Although Sharan had been a researcher at the National Judicial College, had been a parent education facilitator, and had worked in broadcast journalism, much of her past employment had been secretarial. Working as a secretary once again, she was beginning to feel stifled by the confines of repetitive daily tasks.

An opportunity to work together presented itself, and when Sharan joined Frank as his assistant it was an exciting time for both of us—a time of discovery and of learning the art of working together. In only a few weeks we became a creative team, efficient and highly productive. It took us no time at all to learn the value of two brains and two sets of eyes focusing on a single creative endeavor. And through our teamwork we learned to work together as equals.

Once again in her career, Sharan was feeling challenged and stimulated, excited each morning at the prospect of what the new day would bring. The only thing marring our happiness was the knowledge that our employer was becoming increasingly critical of our emerging work style. It was foreign to him to watch two individuals working as closely and cooperatively as we did. To his mind, our sitting side by side at the same computer terminal, writing a catalog, or art-directing photo sessions together seemed a duplication of effort. He could not understand, nor did we ever have time to demonstrate, just how efficient our working style was becoming.

In addition, while most of the staff was supportive of our working relationship, a few people felt intimidated or threatened by what they perceived could become a power base. It was inevitable that one day an impasse would be reached.

The morning that impasse materialized, we were fired together in a single breath. We both felt, simultaneously, shock and liberation—shock because it is demoralizing to be terminated, and liberation in being released from a situation that was becoming increasingly uncomfortable.

But it was only Frank who felt a sense of guilt. He had been the one who had pressed a critical issue to the wall, which had resulted in our termination. Sharan had still been experiencing the exhilaration of her new career, and Frank felt that his actions had robbed her of something she might never again attain.

Happily for us both, our feeling of liberation was accompanied by the sense of a new beginning, and while we were still clearing out our desks Frank proposed that we found our own advertising agency. "I don't ever want to work for someone else again—and I don't ever want to work without you."

Working out of our living room, we spent the next three months planning and launching our new venture. Today Barnett/Associates operates out of pleasant offices in Aptos, California, overlooking a redwood forest. Our firm specializes in producing collaterals—marketing and sales materials, technical seminars and articles, as well as computer and software documentation and packaging—for some of Silicon Valley's largest high-tech firms. Although the computer industry occupies most of our creative energies, our projects have included the creation of brochures and annual reports for nonprofit community organizations, state political initiatives, and national and international charities. As with so many other entrepreneurial couples, if outside circumstances had not intervened, the impetus would not have been there for us to begin our lives as copreneurs.

Our career in high-tech advertising is a far cry from anything we dreamed of during our formal training; and certainly nothing during our previous careers foretold that we would one day be sitting together at a corporate client's conference table discussing a computer product launch. Our story of happenstance is not so very different from the stories of other copreneurs. Almost all of the couples we interviewed for *Working Together* began their working lives in careers quite different from the businesses they now own and operate together.

IT'S TIME TO MAKE THE MUSTARD

Chance and external circumstances played significant roles in the decision of Liz and Nick Thomas to become copreneurs. Today, rising national sales of their gourmet mustards and condiments have taken them from their kitchen to an 8400-square-foot manufacturing plant in Wyndmoor, Pennsylvania.

The phenomenal success of Chalif Inc. in the speciality food industry is an inspiration and model for small gourmet companies seeking to prove that the American dream is still alive. For sixteen years, the Thomases prepared batches of mustard for Christmas gifts. Their recipe had been passed down from Liz's uncle, Edward Chalif, whose father, a great ballet master, had fled from Tsarist Russia with his family—and with the now-famous mustard recipe sewn securely in the hem of his wife's dress.

Since 1906, friends had urged three generations of Chalifs to sell their great mustard. In 1965, Liz and Nick received family permission to market the product, with the stipulation that the recipe be kept secret. Yet, in spite of continued encouragement to enter the marketplace, it wasn't until 1981 that the Thomases finally founded Chalif Inc.

In that year, Nick and Liz were out of work and racked with worry about mounting bills. After a twenty-year career in the insurance industry, Nick had taken a gamble and joined a new business venture. Unfortunately, recession, high interest rates, and insufficient capitalization resulted in the failure of the project, and Nick found himself unemployed for the first time in their lives together. Liz, who had not worked since their marriage, found part-time work as a medical secretary. However, her salary was not sufficient to cover their living expenses. It was a depressing and stressful period for the entire family. As Liz tells their story,

It really was an awful situation. I was going to church every morning just to be in a place where I could recapture my sanity. I'm not any kind of a religious fanatic—believe me—you must understand that first off. Nick's mother had just died the year before and in church, when I would pray for a turn in our fortunes I would feel her presence.

The last afternoon we were with her, Nick had said, "You know, Mom, you're going to see the Lord a lot sooner than I will. I've been having some career problems and it would be really nice if you'd put in a good word for me because I'm really trying hard." The last thing his mother said to him was, "I will, honey." And whenever I was in church, I truly felt Nick's mother was with me.

I would go home to Nick and say, "I feel like your mother is trying to get through and tell me something, and this crazy idea keeps coming into my head that we should be making the mustard!" Nick would laugh, "Liz, do you know how ridiculous that is? Do you know how many jars of mustard it would take to get us out of this financial mess?" and I would say, "I know, but I have this strong feeling."

Well, it happened every day and the more I would resist, the more I felt she was saying to me, "You dummy, you're praying for help and I'm telling you what to do! If you would just do what you *should* be doing, everything will be all right."

Finally, one night, sitting at the table with a pile of bills, and not enough money to pay them—we were down literally to our last two hundred dollars—I said, "This isn't going to satisfy anybody. Why don't we take this money, get some labels and jars, and just try to market the mustard?" At this, Nick threw up his hands and said, "Okay, I can't fight you *and* my mother. But we're not going to put one more cent into this—just the two hundred dollars and that's it!"

The rest of the Chalif story is history. Chalif's gourmet condiments, including an enticing variety of mustards, mayonnaises, sauces, and dips, can now be found from coast to coast on the shelves of some of the country's finest gourmet food stores. Like so many copreneurs, Liz and Nick have found success in an enterprise neither would have dreamed of starting if circumstances had not intervened in their lives.

SOMETIMES A BUSINESS FINDS YOU

During our interviews we encountered instances where it appeared that a business opportunity just seemed to come out of nowhere. Many copreneurs established enterprises as the result of a conscious process. Other businesses seem to have been just waiting in the wings for a chance to appear—and once they entered the scene, there was no stopping them! These enterprises have almost literally swept their founders off their feet, turning their lives completely around.

Growing up, Gayle, whose mother hated baking, recalls her
childhood baking attempts with horror. "My baking experiences were very bad—I was almost electrocuted one time
baking!"

In 1971 Gayle was introduced to her future husband, Joe
Ortiz. It was an instant attraction, and when Joe decided to
return to law school in another city, Gayle joined him. Within a
year, however, Joe, listening to his real feelings, abandoned his
legal studies once and for all. "I hated law school. I quit after
the first year because I hated it, and I quit again that second
year."

The couple then worked together for a time painting houses
in San Francisco. But that business was not a success and Joe
and Gayle parted company. Gayle still remembers her excitement when she once again heard from Joe, a few months later.
"I got a call from him asking if he could visit for the weekend. I
was ecstatic! Within three months we were married."

Nothing in their life at that time indicated that they would
one day be the owners of one of the most successful businesses
in their community, an enterprise that would sweep both of
them along in its growth. They spent the next few years working apart, Joe as a house painter and musician and Gayle as a
waitress. As their work schedules began to separate them, they
felt themselves growing further and further apart. During this
time, Gayle recalls,

> Our lives had been so separate that our relationship was just sort of
> falling away beneath us. And then Joe brought home a brochure
> from a cooking school in San Francisco. He handed it to me,
> saying, "I bid on painting a cooking school this week and they
> asked me if I wanted to barter cooking classes for part of the
> contract. Why don't you look these over and see if you might want
> to take a course?" My eyes just zeroed in on this French pastry
> course. I read over the course outline and said, "French pastries,
> this is it!"
>
> Joe never did paint the school, but I took one course from a very
> inspiring woman, and then another, and another. I became com-
> pletely enthralled and started baking French cakes at home. I had a

lot of failures, but it was a vision. I didn't know what I was going to do with it until I discovered croissants. I had read about them in *Gourmet Magazine*, but at that time there were no croissants in the Santa Cruz area where we were living—not even in San Francisco.

I started making croissants, and I'll be darned if it didn't work. I just baked and baked, wholesaling them out of the house. I was still working as a waitress in the daytime, but at night I would make the dough to bake in the morning, pop them in the oven while I dressed, and deliver them on my way to work.

When Joe and I added up my receipts and discovered that I had made three thousand dollars out of our kitchen in just one year, we were shocked. I know that's not very much, but when it got to the point where I was ordering hundred pound sacks of flour and sixty-eight pounds of butter at once, Joe said, "Isn't it about time you got this business out of the house?" We opened our bakery ten years ago with an offering of just ten items, and earned sixty dollars on that first day. Now we serve a thousand customers a day and have seventy-five employees. I don't think we envisioned this, but I never doubted we'd succeed.

Joe's involvement in Gayle's Bakery in Capitola, California came as a result of his half-hearted participation in Gayle's project. On the advice of Gayle's father, who owned a restaurant-equipment business, the couple realized that their bakery would have to include bread as well as pastries. And, since Gayle didn't enjoy making bread, Joe agreed to help out for a time,

I said I would bake the bread for one year—just until Gayle got started. Then I'd go off and do what I wanted to do. I still worked as a house painter, and we were getting up at about two or three in the morning to bake. But a funny thing happened—I started to enjoy baking. Then, our first trip to Europe really turned me around. After I discovered what French bread was supposed to look and taste like I flipped over from wanting to get out of the bakery to really wanting involvement. Also, I saw it was a success and figured our combined energies were making it happen.

Once I got involved it wasn't work any more, it was a pursuit—a creative process. And it became an ego thing, too, because so many people were commenting on how much they liked our bread. I had no idea the bakery was going to take off like it did. To me, it was just going to be Gayle's little pastry shop.

Gayle's Bakery and Rosticceria, an Italian-style deli the Ortizes opened adjacent to their bakery in 1983, are institutions to their thirty thousand devoted customers. From their original 850-square-foot French bakery to its present configuration occupying 3200 square-feet, their enterprise now grosses over two million dollars annually. Instead of the hundred-pound sacks of flour that Gayle used to heft into their home, the business now consumes over twenty thousand pounds of flour, four thousand pounds of sugar, twenty-six thousand eggs, twenty-five hundred pounds of butter and seventeen hundred pounds of chocolate—in just a single month!

Although Joe and Gayle's enterprise was begun spontaneously, and they admit to having been naive at its inception, they have certainly gained appreciable knowledge, sophistication, and expertise as they and their business have grown together. From the beginning, the passion that they held for their bakery is characteristic of other copreneurs who have also "been found" by their businesses.

CHANGING CAREERS TOGETHER

Most of the couples we interviewed are now engaged in careers that have little or no relation to their past working lives. Some are pursing lifelong dreams, while others have discovered new dimensions in their own capabilities as well as professional strengths that have emerged as a result of their copreneurial experiences.

Ted and Joyce Rice are the cofounders of T.J. Cinnamons, the nation's largest specialty bakery chain. Their franchise operation, with over two hundred bakeries across the country, is as different from the single French bakery run by Joe and Gayle Ortiz as it is from their own previous careers. Before founding their company, which *Venture Magazine* in 1988 named the number one growth franchise in America, Ted had been an award-winning television news cameraman for twenty-three years, and for seventeen years Joyce had taught fifth grade. Their organization, which began as a part-time business in a mobile bakery, exploded in just four years into a fifty-million-dollar-a-year business headquartered in Kansas City, Missouri.

The remarkable story of the Rices' new career together is one of hard work, risk taking, and a fiery entrepreneurial spirit. It began in 1982 when they took a three-month sabbatical from their respective careers. During their time off they sailed three thousand miles on Lake Superior at the leisurely pace of less than five miles per hour. That time out from their busy lives allowed them to reflect and examine their future. At the end of the cruise, the Rices had reached the conclusion that they could do anything they wanted—even start their own business. And they agreed that, regardless of the nature of their new venture, it would have to allow them to work together.

After exploring businesses from delicatessens to craft shops, they were struck with the idea of a mobile bakery while attending a state fair where they encountered a vendor selling cinnamon rolls. Ted spent the next winter designing a twenty-foot mobile bakery. In the meantime, he recalls, "Joyce designed a cinnamon roll that was unsurpassed," an eight-ounce, softball-sized gourmet delight.

With the mobile bakery complete and Joyce's recipe perfected, the couple took to the road, introducing their fresh-baked cinnamon rolls at fairs and festivals in twelve midwestern states. Crowds gathered to buy the cinnamon rolls hot from the oven, and the reputation of T.J. Cinnamons gourmet cinnamon rolls grew. Soon Joyce gave up her teaching career to pursue their new venture year-round. In January of 1985, Ted joined Joyce full-time, they opened their first permanent bakery location, and a new chapter began in their incredible success story.

FROM PALETTE TO PALATE

Other couples we met recounted equally remarkable tales of their career changes. Before becoming restaurateurs and master chefs, Johanne Killeen and George Germon were artists, follow-ing quite different career paths. Johanne was a professional photographer and George a sculptor and architect, teaching at the Rhode Island School of Design in Providence, Rhode Island. While they were searching for a means to support their careers as full-time artists, their lives took an unexpected turn. Look-ing back at the changes in their lives since the decision to open their first restaurant, Al Forno, George told us how they had originally envisioned their project.

> We thought we would like to do a little lunch-time operation, just to give us a weekly income and support us as artists. However, when we got into it, within one week, we knew we loved it. Each of us gave up our professions, devoting ourselves totally to the restau-rant. We decided that in order to do anything well, you have to just concentrate on that one thing. So we made that commitment and went with it.
>
> Then we made up our minds that we were going to be recognized because we felt that would make us grow. After that decision, the rest was easy—easy because every time we received more recogni-tion we wanted to go further. And to keep that recognition com-ing, we worked even harder.
>
> Our backgrounds have been very helpful to our success. Probably one of the most important things about what we do is that we begin creating each new dish from a visual approach, and only then do we decide how it should taste and what we want the balances to be.

Both George and Johanne bring many talents from their artistic pasts to their present enterprises. Johanne's skills as an artist and photographer have enhanced her abilities as a nation-ally renowned chef and enriched the presentation of their unique gourmet creations. George's architectural and mechani-cal skills come into play time and time again as the couple refine and expand their businesses.

The couple's innovative recipes and cooking techniques, which employ wood-burning grills and ovens, as well as the intimate and welcoming atmosphere of both Al Forno and Lucky's, are the result of their design collaborations and talents. George discussed the significant contributions their experiences bring to their enterprises.

Our backgrounds are very helpful, because they always bring something into the restaurant. It also enriches the vocabulary of what we are doing. I think that everything you do and everything you've been adds to what you're making and building. In every project you draw from your past—it's like a little computer.

I don't think there's a project we can't undertake. Sometimes we look at things and feel overwhelmed, but when we really set our minds to accomplish it, we can just do it! We both have varied enough backgrounds that we can pull the thing together and we have enough resources here in Providence that I would say ninety-nine percent of the time we could make any project work that we want to.

Review after review from *The New York Times* to *Food & Wine* give testimony to the outstanding culinary achievements of these copreneurs. And those of us fortunate enough to have had our palates graced by George and Johanne's gastronomical delights join the endorsement of *Bon Appetit* reviewer Richard Sax, who wrote, "Al Forno and Lucky's are two of my favorite places in the world to eat."

FROM CITY LIFE TO COUNTRY LIVING

Another couple who successfully changed careers together are David and Suzanne Brown of Plantation Farm Camp, Inc. How these copreneurs arrived at their decision to effect a total change in their professional careers, their personal lives, and the lives of their children is a story filled with risks, challenges, and love.

As the Browns spun their tale, we sat comfortably protected from a gray Mendocino Coast drizzle in their newly constructed farm house, a replica of the original Plantation house that stood on that same site for over a hundred years. From time to time our meeting was punctuated by visits from the Browns' ten-year-old son and six-year-old twin daughters, who would tiptoe into the living room to report on the happenings about the farm.

In 1983, when David and Suzanne received a call from Abe

and Eve Crittenden, the elderly copreneurs who founded Plantation Farm Camp in the early fifties, it took David "literally just a minute and a half," to know that he wanted to accept the Crittenden's offer to sell Plantation to them. At that time, the Browns were living happily in Fort Collins, Colorado where Suzanne taught junior high school and David was a professor of animal physiology. As David remembers,

> We were clearly at a crossroads. Although I loved what I was doing, the university system was making greater and greater demands on my time. As a young professor I was lucky to be successful in a new field, the investigation of male contraceptives. But I had moved away from whole-animal research, my first love, to lab work—working with a lot of cells, cultures, and genetic manipulations.
>
> I was faced with the opportunity to move to Ohio State University and continue my research. And yet I knew that wasn't really what I wanted to be doing. The time required by my work was keeping me away from my family more and more, and I was not willing to give up being with my children. So I had to discover how I would be able to do something more in conjunction with the family, rather than continue on my present course.
>
> My research was definitely separating me from the people I love most, and would eventually move all of us away from the roots we were establishing in Colorado. Above all, I wanted to be part of raising my children, not just lost to a laboratory somewhere.

During our interviews we were able to obtain two views of the same events. Often those perceptions were similar, but occasionally the emotions experienced by each partner at a given time in their history were very different. That is not to suggest that both individuals were not fully aware of what the other was thinking and feeling. Suzanne's reflections on that period of their life together illustrate her recognition of what David was experiencing as well as of her own needs and feelings at that time.

> I had just started back to get a master's degree and we had a great home, great friends, and I had a great job. With two sources of income, while we were not wealthy, we were very comfortable. But I also knew David was not really happy and that the handwriting

was on the wall. Jobs for David were looming out there in some pretty icky places!

And then one rainy February night we got this call from Abe and Eve. They often called just to chat, but at the end of this conversation they said, "Oh, by the way, how would you like to purchase Plantation?" In their seventies, they had come to the realization that they just couldn't keep up with the work of the farm anymore.

I guess my first thought was that I really didn't want to be isolated, living that far out in the country. And yet, if we couldn't stay in Fort Collins, there was something very exciting about being on our own in a really wonderful place. Like David, I felt the same affinity for Plantation—the magic of this place and the importance it has played in our lives, and here was an opportunity to bring our children into that picture as well. Our life has been so connected with Plantation and the place meant so much to us that it felt like it was just *meant* to happen.

We sat down and listed the pros and cons—what we would get out of doing this and what we would lose. Since the camp had been closed for some time, we didn't even know if we could reestablish a clientele. And if we could not run the summer camp, what else would we be able to do to earn enough to live?

About two weeks later we flew out and looked at the place. We could see that things had begun to deteriorate and there was a lot of work to be done. The old farmhouse needed renovation and the fences were sorely in need of repair. We discussed finances with Abe and Eve. They really wanted us to have Plantation, and because of this they made it financially possible.

When we made our final decision—right at the beginning—we approached running Plantation as a couple. In fact, an important part of the farm's history is that it has always been run by a couple.

The Browns have never regretted their decision to purchase the farm. In listening to them recount the challenges of their first year, told with such enthusiasm and humor, it is evident that the decision to bring about a complete change in their careers and lives is one that is working for the entire family. And, as a result of their hard work, their initial concern that they might not be able to rebuild the summer camp program has proved to be groundless.

Although David's training in animal physiology and Suzanne's teaching career certainly bring essential skills to their

new life and copreneurial enterprise, the career changes they
have committed to are a world away from the secure academic
and city environments that characterized their lives in Fort
Collins, Colorado.

A DOUBLE DOSE OF DOCS

At the beginning of this chapter we stated that many of us
find ourselves in careers that are a result of happenstance. Some
of us, however, actually plot out our professional lives and
follow those plans. And sometimes those plans expand into a
copreneurial enterprise. Bruce Handloff's chiropractic training
resulted in the establishment of the practice that he shares today
with his wife, Masami. In Reno, Nevada, we discovered another
couple whose education and training allow them to work together in their joint enterprise.

While traveling through Reno, we picked up a copy of the
Reno Gazette-Journal with the intriguing headline, "Double
Dose of Docs." Over breakfast at a roadside cafe, we read about
Drs. Sharon and Tom Dose, young veterinarians who own and
operate the Kings Road Pet Hospital. That article led to a
delightful interview with the Doses just a week later.

Sharon and Tom met while attending veterinary college in
Iowa. They graduated in 1980 at the top of their class, with
Sharon as valedictorian. Just two days after their graduation
ceremony they were married. They look back at the time sur-
rounding those two ceremonies with recognition of the stress
they were undergoing—in a period of only ten days they graduated, got married, took state and national veterinary board
exams, and packed their belongings for the move from Iowa to
Las Vegas, where each had a job waiting.

After two years in Las Vegas, where they were practicing at
separate clinics, their grueling schedules had taken their toll.
The long hours, which had them passing one another like
caravans in the desert, brought the Doses to the realization that
it was time to return to Iowa where they could practice veterinary medicine together. Tom tells how the two of them went to

work for his cousin, who was building a new clinic in Davenport, Iowa, not far from Tom's home town.

> My cousin thought only in terms of hiring a male veterinarian, and since I just happened to have a wife who was also a veterinarian, he felt she should do everything in her power to help me do my job. Sharon was paid only when she was working under his supervision, and the hours she worked with me didn't count. My cousin saw it as just part of the family putting in the effort for the business, and justified Sharon's lack of compensation with the rationalization that I was earning enough to support a family of two.
>
> What he didn't recognize was that we were two professional veterinarians who *both* wanted to work. It was also part of the bias among veterinarians that a woman can't really be in a profession where cows, pigs, and horses have to be treated.

Having graduated at the top of her class, Sharon found the experience of not being able to practice her chosen profession full-time to be frustrating, ego deflating, and eventually intolerable. But when she applied for positions elsewhere in the community, she soon discovered that as the wife of a practicing veterinarian, in spite of her own credentials, she was viewed by other veterinary clinics as being married to "the competition."

After a year and a half of trying to find work within commuting distance, Sharon loaded up the couple's car and began a nine-month odyssey to find a situation in which both she and Tom could work. Her search finally ended in Reno, Nevada. In the meantime, Tom had continued to practice with his cousin, joining Sharon whenever possible on weekends. During those difficult months of separation, Tom expressed understanding for Sharon's plight.

> I'm a patient kind of guy. It was clear to me that as a veterinarian Sharon was at a far greater disadvantage to ever be asked to buy into a practice than I was. Between us, I was the one who would have that opportunity and could create a situation where we could work together, and I was always working toward that goal.
>
> At the same time, working for my cousin, Sharon was suffering tremendous frustrations. Her paycheck was not a reflection of all she was doing, and to her that diminished her sense of self-worth.

I'm sure that's part of the reason she took off on her nine-month voyage through the West to find a place for both of us to work and live. And here I was, sitting back in Iowa feeling rather put upon. I wanted to be a large-animal practitioner, but I had married a woman veterinarian and there was no place in Iowa that could absorb two doctors into one practice.

Sharon ended up finding a job here in Reno. I'd fly out about every second or third month and we'd have a weekend together. It was tough on our relationship, to say the least. And I think that's when we set the priorities that it doesn't matter who we work for, or where we are, or what we do—as long as we're together and it's mutually beneficial to both of us and to our relationship. There's nothing more important than that.

So, in the end, here's this poor old country doctor who really hadn't planned on working on dogs and cats, loading up this blankety-blank U-Haul to drive two thousand miles in one hundred and twenty degree heat to treat dogs and cats in the desert with his bonehead wife.

The Dose's original plan had been to locate a practice in which they could both eventually become partners. However, Sharon and Tom soon came to the realization that it would be short-sighted to buy into a practice when the two of them could start their own veterinary clinic together. When they finally opened the doors of their pet hospital they had invested every-thing they had in equipment and supplies. On that first day, Drs. Sharon and Tom Dose treated seven patients. "That," Tom remembers, "was magnificent. We'd go days when we saw only two people. And now we see anywhere from forty-five to over sixty animals in just a single day."

FROM ENTREPRENEURING TO COPRENEURING

Not all of the copreneurs we encountered began working together at the outset of their businesses. In some instances the business was founded by both partners, with one taking the helm while the other continued on in outside employment, lending a supportive role. In other cases the establishment of a business was clearly the accomplishment of a single individual who was joined by a partner at a later date. One such entrepreneur who later became a copreneur is Irene Cohen, of Irene Cohen Personnel Services in New York City.

We met with Irene and her husband, Sy, at their Fifth Avenue office, directly across the street from the New York Public Library. Irene, a petite, dynamic woman, sat at a large executive desk in her attractively appointed office, while Sy positioned himself next to his wife in a side chair.

The Cohens, a delightful couple who have been married for thirty-four years, today operate a successful company with two offices in downtown Manhattan, a Wall Street office and headquarters on Fifth Avenue. Married at the age of eighteen, Irene did not enter the workplace until her early thirties, when she became an employment counselor. She worked in that first job for only three years before she decided to open her own personnel agency.

Originally she intended to start that venture with her former employer as a partner. That plan fell through, however, when her prospective partner backed out at the last minute. Undaunted, Irene forged ahead, opening Irene Cohen Personnel Services in 1974.

> I opened in the middle of a recession and everyone was telling me I was crazy to do it. But Sy was very supportive and said to go ahead and try it. At that time what I thought to myself was, "Everybody should have a chance to fail and I've never had that chance." Sy and I were married while I was still a teen-ager and I had never really done anything up until that time. I was thirty-two when I started my first job and thirty-six when I opened this agency.
>
> At that time, Sy had his own company and was ready to move us out of the city again, this time to Pennsylvania. But we had already moved several times and I didn't want to again. I'd been in business six months and it had gotten very big very fast. It was incredible. I said to Sy, "Look, so we won't make a lot of money for a few years. Let's stay in New York." And he agreed. It was a reverse situation, with the husband consenting to stay put for the wife's career.

Irene and Sy each have their own carefully delineated areas of responsibility and authority. And although Irene was alone in the company's initial start-up, she concedes that it was Sy who was responsible for the growth that took the company beyond the point of just a fledgling operation.

One day Sy said to me, "There is some office space available downstairs on the second floor. You just have to look at it." and I said, "I'm not moving. I'm very happy." He said, "But it's bigger." And my answer to that was, "I don't want to be bigger. I read the *Harvard Business Review*, and I know what will happen—you get bigger, then you die, because you can't handle it. And things are wonderful just the way they are."

Then the next month Sy approached the subject again. And I said, "I'm not looking at it. Forget it!" But not long after that, returning to our office one day from lunch, I saw that our reception area and lobby were packed with applicants.

"Sy," I said, "this is ridiculous—we don't have enough room for these people." Taking me by the arm, Sy said, "Come downstairs, I want to show you something." We went down there and saw this space and my reaction was immediate. "Sy, I must have it!" And he patiently replied, "Irene, I told you about this space months ago. Now they've probably got someone already signed up." "I don't care," I said, "you've got to get it for me Sy. It's perfect."

So Sy talked to our landlord and, although there was someone interested in the space, we got it and that started an important change. If it hadn't been for Sy pushing me, we'd probably still be upstairs on the twelfth floor operating a small agency.

When Irene first established the company, the Cohens' initial investment had been a manageable $5000, and the rent for that first 900-square-foot office was just $6000 per year. Moving into larger quarters meant a commitment to a minimum of 3600 square feet—four times the space originally occupied—and an increase in their annual rent to $54,000. It was a move, however, that Sy had the vision to understand was necessary for the growth and survival of their company.

For Irene, a huge psychological hurdle had to be overcome. She stressed that for women in business, learning to take risks and to make those quantum leaps, so necessary for business growth, is one of the most difficult and challenging tasks. Irene had found the initial risk of opening her own agency anxiety-producing, and she had little desire to recreate those feelings in the pit of her stomach.

Yet Irene took that first quantum leap, and has learned from it the importance of risk-taking. Together, she and Sy have grown and expanded their agency, which today occupies 15,000 square feet. And while it had taken an initial investment of just $5000 to open the agency, launching their Employee Leasing Division required $500,000! Clearly, Irene has become comfortable with confronting and taking risk.

Irene Cohen Personnel Services is now among the top three or four independent personnel agencies in New York City. The Cohens' enterprise has divisions for temporary placement, permanent placement, word processing and computer training, and employee leasing. For Irene, the move from entrepreneur to copreneur—joining forces with Sy—has resulted in the growth and expansion of their company.

TAKING AND SHARING CONTROL

The couples we interviewed across the country have little in common with each another—with the one notable exception of having made the choice to enter into a copreneurial relationship. Each of their twenty-four-hour-a-day partnerships has resulted from their individual decisions to take and share control of their lives together rather than to face the daily battles and uncertainties of the workplace alone.

The nature of their friendships and their mutual respect are the basic building blocks around which they have structured their personal and working relationships. For these couples, copreneuring has been their response to taking control in a confusing, troubled, and volatile economic world. Equally important, for many it has been a reaffirmation of the importance of strong personal ties and traditional family values. Thus the copreneurial movement is a resurgence of commitment to the concept of a family unit pulling together.

Moreover, all of these couples have learned and grown together in their business enterprises. Very few had previous entrepreneurial experience, and yet all found the courage to leap from dependence on outside employment to the far less secure ground of owning and being responsible for their own business endeavors. The risk and the courage to accept that risk are common characteristics that we discovered in all of the copreneurs we met.

The impetus to found their businesses was in some cases forced upon these individuals as a result of external circumstances. For other couples, the opportunity appeared out of the blue. Some began their ventures together and still others were joined at a later date by their partners. For most, becoming a copreneur was not only a new and exciting adventure, it also entailed accepting the challenge and opportunity that a new career afforded.

Looking back on their enterprises, their beginnings, and where their businesses are today, none of these copreneurs could possibly have anticipated the complexities with which they would have to deal, nor the successes they would attain. Significantly, most did not embark on their journeys with formal business plans securely in hand; nor did they take the luxury of spending months or even years in thought and planning for their future endeavor.

While common wisdom suggests that businesses that start off with a plan are more likely to succeed, in fact those plans are rarely followed. It would be presumptuous to assume that a world filled with competition, capricious customers, and the unexpected will perform dutifully to even the best of business plans. And any plan, after all, is only the culmination of hopes, desires, and a generous mixture of whatever limited knowledge its creator possesses.

Business plans aside, the copreneurs we met are all action-oriented individuals who, once their decision was made, seized the opportunity and made it happen. As you recall, it took David Brown of Plantation "literally just a minute and a half" to reach a life- and career-changing decision. Our own decision to establish an advertising agency was thrust upon us unexpectedly one September morning, and within minutes we had agreed to face the world together as copreneurs.

Within a week after beginning a business that George and Johanne thought would be "just a little lunch-time operation," the decision was made to devote themselves totally to becoming master chefs and restaurateurs. Ted and Joyce Rice found inspiration for their first mobile bakery at a fair, and Joe and Gayle Ortiz's bakery "found" them. Nick Thomas, down to his last $200, simply threw up his hands in resignation, yielding to Liz's vision to make their first batch of mustard. And with that, those couples embarked on new business adventures, gaining and sharing control of their lives.

It has been our experience, and the experience of other couples in business together, that when an opportunity presents itself you either act on it immediately or the opportunity will pass you by. In spite of the apparent randomness involved in establishing a business, and the high number of copreneurs whose enterprises demanded dramatic career changes, the couples we investigated each brought just the right combination of talents and knowledge from their past lives to bear on their new business ventures.

Working together is indeed a unique dance. When executed correctly, it is a dance in which neither partner has the absolute lead. Once a couple makes the decision to establish a copreneurial relationship, the track taken is of little significance. What matters is that both partners are committed to being on that same track, and proceed down it with a clear picture of where they are traveling together.

PART TWO

Working Together As Copreneurs

Copreneurs have learned that together they possess the ability to achieve their goals. They realize that without "ourselves," the concept of "myself" is without meaning.

CHAPTER

4

Find Your Niche and Fill It

Looking at a copreneurial relationship from the outside, people often have the question, "How do the two of you work together?" This should not be interpreted as "How can you stand working together?" It is instead asked out of genuine curiosity and a desire to understand. In spite of the growing numbers of couples working together, copreneuring remains relatively invisible in the business world. And when people encounter a couple who live and work together twenty-four hours a day, the question just naturally arises.

Setting out on our interviews, we knew that one of the answers we wanted to obtain from each of the couples we would meet was a response to that very question. While the question itself is broad and open-ended in nature, we discovered that the answers, however diverse, could all be grouped into two distinct categories—those partners who work together assuming separate responsibilities, and those who share the same responsibilities.

Once you have made the decision to become a copreneur, and once you and your partner are traveling together on the same track, a process begins in which your individual roles in your new enterprise become defined. Similarly, the already established roles in your personal life will become redefined.

CAPITALIZE ON YOUR RELATIONSHIP

When you and your partner join forces and set up a business together, you must decide how your relationship is to be viewed by the outside world. Will you present an all-business façade? Will your customers or clients be aware of your unique and special relationship? Or will you hide your personal relationship from those with whom you do business?

We have met a few couples in the business world who have assumed closet relationships—some to protect their positions, and others who felt it necessary to keep their personal and business lives separate. We have met only one true entrepreneurial couple, however, who kept their marriage a secret from those outside their firm. And that relationship, at our last contact, was disintegrating into a divorce.

When we first hit the streets, introducing our newly established agency to prospective clients, we were pleasantly surprised to find ourselves quickly racking up accounts. One of our early prospects, a high-tech firm loaded with venture capital and on the verge of its first product launch, requested that our agency give a presentation to its board of directors. The day before that meeting, the marketing director, a pleasant woman who very much wanted to use our services, cornered us in her office, offering her advice.

> I really want to work with you. Your stuff is just great. But it's too bad that you both have the same last name and that it's printed on your business cards. This company is very male dominated and if the two of you are at the meeting tomorrow they'll see you as a small Mom and Pop shop. It's my suggestion that just one of you come and give the presentation.

This was the first time the term Mom and Pop had been used in the context of our own enterprise and, as novice copreneurs, we were flabbergasted. We had made a conscious decision at the time of our marriage to use the same last name, as a statement about our feelings, our commitment, and who we are. To be told that this was a handicap triggered much discussion long into the evening. Finally we knuckled under—Frank would give the pitch alone.

We had prepared the campaign and visual aids for the presentation together, and when it came time for Frank to leave for that meeting, Sharan's curiosity would not let him go alone. There was no way she could delay knowing the outcome, and since she couldn't attend the presentation she rode along in the car and sat reading a book in the parking lot. Two hours later an exhausted Frank returned to the car. His response to Sharan's "How did it go?" was immediate and filled with resolve. "I'll never do that alone again. It's not that I couldn't handle it—it's just that there was so much you would have contributed. We both worked on this and you deserved to be there too. We're partners and a team and that's just the way we're always going to work from now on."

As it turned out, this was one of the few presentations where we struck out. Ironically, and perhaps prophetically, the woman we were working with, to Frank's surprise, had not been in on that board meeting. She was soon sidelined into another department and eventually out of the company.

We had learned our first lesson—we are a team, and we always work together. If a prospective client can't work with us as an entrepreneurial couple at the outset, we feel the odds are fairly high that other problems would soon loom on the horizon. As we have become more comfortable with our relationship in public, we have moved from downplaying our marriage to even capitalizing upon it, on rare occasions.

Not long ago Frank found himself in a corner during a particularly difficult meeting with a client while presenting a national advertising campaign. We had written and designed the "perfect" ad, which the client loved—except they were insisting that we "just change the headline." We both knew that to "just change the headline" as suggested would alter the entire meaning of the campaign. The client was adamant and Frank, realizing that we were on an extremely tight schedule and facing a rewrite and possible redesign, was pressing to retain the ad as presented. The timely launching of the campaign was in jeopardy, and the meeting was getting hot.

During meetings one of us will occasionally signal the other with a look or a nudge beneath the table; when this happens, neither of us visually or verbally acknowledges the communication. However, this meeting was falling apart and the discussion needed a quick turn. So when Frank felt Sharan's not-so-gentle tap on his shin, he leapt at the opportunity to turn the meeting around. Stopping in midsentence he turned to Sharan, saying, "Did you kick me? I can't believe it! I thought we had a pact!"

The clients were now fully focused on the two of us. Turning back to them, Frank asked, "Did you see that? She kicked me! And nothing moved above the waist." By this time, they were in stitches, laughing and wiping their eyes. With this unanticipated interruption, we were able to change the tone of the discussion and bring the meeting back on track again.

Much-needed relief had been provided and we had used our marital status to bring about a desired effect with a client. This is certainly not something we choose to do very often, but on that occasion it proved to be an effective technique. From this meeting we learned a valuable lesson: that there are instances in which we, as copreneurs, *can* capitalize on the most personal aspect of our relationship—our marriage—even when our public persona normally is designed to downplay our private life together. It was important for us to realize that the world does not end when we publicly acknowledge our personal relationship.

Other copreneurs have also learned the value of having outsiders accept the equality that exists between them. Drs. Tom and Sharan Dose are equally capable of caring for any animal, and yet some of their clients express a preference for one or the other of them. They make every effort to accommodate their clients; however, a preference for one of the doctors does not always fit conveniently into the hospital's schedule. And when the health of the other animals is put at risk, Tom becomes emphatic.

If somebody comes in and wants to dictate the policy of our hospital so that it suits them, I can't tolerate that. When they say they won't see one of us and we've got to flip-flop our whole schedule, it's really not worth it. Usually it's for something like a rabies shot or because some people perceive men as being rougher and not as sympathetic with their little pet. They want a lady because "the lady will be more gentle with my cat." So if Sharon gets bitten or scratched, then it's "Oh, poor lady doctor." And if I get bitten or scratched, it's because I've been too rough with their pet.

Our advice to all couples embarking on an enterprise is that they avoid entering into a closet relationship. Rather than hiding the personal nature of your relationship, we urge you to capitalize on it. Your success in your venture will depend upon the honesty that exists between you and your partner, and we do not feel that it is possible to maintain the integrity of your relationship if that honesty does not extend to all people with whom you interact—your employees, clients, and customers. In every instance except one, we have found that our personal working relationship has been accepted without question. And beyond mere acceptance, we believe that our relationship is a valuable asset to our business.

The public image and identity of some of the copreneurial enterprises we met are true reflections of the relationship between the partners. The use of our own last name in our advertising agency, and our titles of president and executive director, reflect the equality of our working relationship. And Ted and Joyce Rice, who *are* the "T" and "J" in T.J. Cinnamons, bill themselves in their marketing as cofounders.

An advertising agency in Phoenix, Arizona has applied a novel twist in identity that sends a clear signal to their clients concerning the equality in their relationship and capabilities by naming their firm "Richardson or Richardson." The "or" in their company name is a tiny but powerful message and was a real stroke of genius by the partners, Valerie and Forrest Richardson, who opened their agency in 1983.

While Sam Edelman admits to building their fashion shoe enterprise around the image of his wife, Libby, their corporate name, Sam & Libby, California, says it all. Their dynamic organization is very much a collaboration between the partners, and reflects the eclectic style of today's modern woman. The fact that Sam's name precedes Libby's was purely a matter of phonics, just as the order of our own names is on the cover of this book. Like ourselves and other copreneurs, the Edelmans view their partnership and intimate relationship as very much a positive asset to their business—an image that has been incorporated into their company's overall marketing strategy.

However, outside the community of copreneurs not everyone views the enterprises of entrepreneurial couples in so positive a light. Traditionally, the venture capitalist community has looked upon the enterprises of husbands and wives with a jaundiced eye. The name of the game for venture capital is the control and ultimate takeover of the companies they back. Therefore the loyalty and strong bonds between the two partners in a copreneurial relationship is viewed negatively by these financiers. No one interested in control wishes to be placed in a minority position. There are some venture capitalists who now recognize the value of two strong partners in a start-up business, and who specialize in financing these enterprises. For most, though, the experience of Sam and Libby Edelman is the norm.

When Libby and I started our business we were introduced to the venture capital community, and we were told it would be very easy to raise money for our new business. We met with one venture capitalist who said he could raise two million dollars for us overnight, whenever we wanted.

So we just took our life savings, everything we could pull together, and started our business, thinking if we ever needed money that there was this thing called a venture capitalist who overnight would give us money. Coming from a very, very large company, we started aggressively with our little business. And one day, about five months after we started, we thought that maybe we needed some money. So we arranged a meeting with the same venture capitalist again. During the meeting he asked many questions about our relationship as a couple, and later we found out that one of the main considerations behind our being turned down was that we are a married couple and that was a negative to the venture capital community. We went to three other venture capitalists, and the story was the same with each of them. Because we are a couple, we were not considered a good risk.

I was in a state of shock because, to me, you get two for the price of one. You're getting the most unbelievable thing in a married couple. One of the biggest problems encountered by entrepreneurs who are not in business as coentrepreneurs is their spouse—because in an entrepreneurial, high-pressure business you must work so hard and devote so much of your life to your venture that if your spouse is concerned about what time you get home for dinner, or how much you travel, or that you only think about your business, there exists a terrible negative in your business.

With a married couple who are both working together, the goal is to be successful. And you're both working toward that goal all the time. It's what you both think about, it's what you talk about in your bed. Our rejection has made me very critical of the venture capital community for not viewing married couples as possessing an enormous amount of potential. As it turned out, we didn't need the venture capitalists at all. If we'd had that extra money it might actually have been to our detriment. Working lean meant working smarter.

THE THREE HUNDRED PERCENT THINK TANK

In the early months of working together, we quickly recognized that we are a potent team. When we accomplished a particularly difficult task or met one more impossible deadline we would quip to ourselves, "Between us we have one helluva good brain." That joking self-deprecation came from our realization that in addition to our strengths, we also have individual weaknesses. And as far too many of us do, we were selling ourselves short.

We all have areas in which we excel, while at the same time harboring inadequacies that we work hard to conceal from the world. And each of us is a whole individual in spite of our flaws, shortcomings, and deficiencies. When we are not part of a team, we find ourselves wasting valuable time doing things we are not good at, rather than concentrating on those areas in which we perform best.

Once we realized that working together allowed us to maximize our talents and minimize our weaknesses, we recognized that because of our working relationship we were each operating at a full one hundred percent. And together, we are more than the sum of our separate parts—not two hundred percent, but three hundred percent!

The synergism between us has resulted in a magnification of our combined abilities. Every project we have completed has clearly been the product of more than just the two of us. Our creations are the result of the synergy that we refer to as *Our Brain* or the *Three Hundred Percent Think Tank*. And that same synergism is at the disposal of all copreneurs, making it possible for couples working together to accomplish the impossible. The concept that a couple working together can produce more than two individuals working separately may be difficult for some to grasp. Yet every entrepreneurial couple we met discussed how they were accomplishing far more together than they ever did working alone.

TO SPECIALIZE OR NOT TO SPECIALIZE

For most couples, the division of labor comes quite naturally as a result of individual capabilities, knowledge, skills, and what each partner brings to the venture from their past. Many copreneurs develop clearly separated areas of responsibility, performing tasks and making decisions independently of their partner, while others elect to run their businesses with the lines of responsibility blurred, sharing the same or similar tasks.

During our interviews we met with many copreneurs who, like ourselves, produce products or provide services while maintaining a work style of shared responsibilities. Other couples support one another by performing in areas of responsibility which, while a necessary part of the whole, fall into quite distinct, specialized realms. As we met with couples we became aware that those copreneurs like ourselves who work together without dividing functions and tasks may be able to do so because of the relatively small size of their organizations. Nonspecialization may, in fact, be a luxury of businesses that are composed only of the two partners, or that operate with a small staff. We did not encounter any large copreneurial enterprise where both partners share tasks equally across the board. Perhaps such interchangeability is not possible when businesses grow beyond the capabilities of just two people and when multiple levels of management evolve within the organization.

Claude Jeanloz, of The Renovator's Supply in Millers Falls, Massachusetts, articulated this observation during our interview with him and his wife, Donna.

> I think that it's very difficult for a couple to run a business together, doing everything, when you get to a certain level and have a lot of employees. In a small establishment, they can both pitch in, telling employees how to run the operation and doing everything. But when you start having other tiers of management involved, everything changes because the managers start playing one against the other and the couple can end up arguing.
>
> It's very rare, I think, that a business of any size is actually run by a couple. If it's run successfully, usually the two individuals have very specific and distinct areas of expertise or responsibility. That's the only way it can really work. Otherwise, it can end up in a divorce with one taking the business and the other going off to do something else, or the company just closes down.
>
> There are large businesses that appear to be run equally by the couple, but I believe that if you dig into it, you'll find one involved in the marketing and the other in running the day-to-day aspects of the business.

In just ten years, the Jeanlozes have built a multi-national corporation centered around the manufacturing and direct-mail sales of reproduction plumbing and lighting fixtures, and speciality door, cabinet, and window hardware. Their full-color catalog is now mailed at a steady rate of fifty thousand each working day—an astounding twelve million annually!

While smallness and specialization are not mutually exclusive, bigness and nonspecialization may indeed be incompatible, or at least impractical in most endeavors. An important distinction in a nonspecialized work style is the difference between *working interchangeably* and *collaborating together.* Couples who collaborate together, sharing projects as well as responsibilities or tasks, seem to do so in enterprises that involve high levels of creativity. Those copreneurs who work on tasks interchangeably, either together or alone, generally operate enterprises in which creativity does not necessarily result in the final product.

To the successful coentrepreneur, the division of labor is never a matter of breaking tasks into small, meaningless units. Rather, we have found that these couples apportion the work between themselves into whole and meaningful areas of responsibility and control, whether or not they elect to divide or share the tasks. Certainly, one of the motivating forces that drives entrepreneurs out of the employment arena and into business for themselves is their desire to identify with an entire product or service and to assume the responsibility for maintaining the standards they themselves have set.

One of the first major decisions you will face as a copreneur will be to choose the working style that is best suited to you and your partner. This involves one basic decision—to work together, sharing tasks and responsibilities, or to divide the elements of your business and work on them separately. You must decide whether your working style will be one of specialization or nonspecialization, and determine whether that style is suited to your personal relationship.

5

When Roles and Tasks Are Shared–Nonspecialization

During meetings with our clients, we are often asked whether it was Frank or Sharan who was responsible for a particular aspect of a project. "Which of you wrote this?" Or "Whose idea was that design?" On occasion, some of our clients find it difficult to understand our total collaborative process. And in spite of our description of how we work together, some people will arbitrarily assign separate roles to each of us. In those cases Frank might become the art director and Sharan the writer; at other times, the roles assigned to each of us might be reversed. We have learned to accept this and understand it is the result of a time in which specialization in the workplace is the norm.

Because of our collaborative work style, we neither take individual credit for a project nor invest our egos in a particular creative function. For us, this collaboration has resulted in a higher level of creativity and productivity, as well as having the added benefit of eliminating competition between us. Thus our competitive energies are focused outside the relationship and can be channeled into our creative endeavors.

Neither of us assumes the dominant role with our clients. During meetings one or the other of us will take the lead, setting the agenda and chairing the session. But if one of us hits a rough spot, the other is always there to quickly step in.

Before meeting with other entrepreneurial couples we had given considerable thought to the way we work together and had come, quite incorrectly, to the assumption that our working style was unique and possibly self-indulgent. Having worked together in a vacuum, like so many other copreneurs, we had not encountered another creative team whose collaborations were brought about through such an intense interaction. We had even wondered on occasion if our working style was inefficient since we always write projects, proof copy, attend press checks, and deal with vendors and clients together. "Wouldn't it be more efficient," we would ask ourselves, "if we didn't always work together?" At the beginning of our enterprise that was, in fact, exactly how we worked.

We began with two computers and two automobiles, believing that having those tools available to each of us would allow us to be twice as productive. It wasn't long, however, before we found ourselves in front of one computer screen again, writing together—and doing it at double speed! We quickly rediscovered a lesson we had learned when first working together as coemployees. By combining our energies in both the creative and production phases of our work, our output more than doubled.

In addition, as our business grew and our working patterns became established, we found ourselves traveling together in the same automobile. Eventually we realized that, for us, two cars merely meant two payments and higher insurance rates. With that we sold the second car, and we've never missed it. Today, parked in its place in the garage is a ping-pong table, which affords the entire family considerably more pleasure than that second set of wheels ever did.

As we began our interviewing process and learned how other copreneurs work together, it became evident that many share our nonspecialized work style, working collaboratively or interchangeably, either alone or together. Those couples who have elected to work in this fashion are engaged in very diverse enterprises—chefs, television producers, stable owners, bookstore operators, photographers, and authors, to name only a few.

We came away from our interviews with the knowledge that our working style was not, after all, either an oddity or an indulgence. It was just one way of working together—a style that works very well for us as well as for many other couples we met.

TWO PARTNERS IN A SINGLE ROLE

Because of their nearly identical professional training and their commitment to operating an efficient clinic, veterinarians Sharon and Tom Dose have established a nonspecialized style of attending to the needs of their patients. While they often work independently of one another in their clinic, they do not divide patients or most responsibilities into *his* and *hers* categories. They each receive and treat patients as their owners bring them into the clinic—an animal may be seen by Tom on one visit and by Sharon on the next.

The only area in which they do specialize is surgery; Sharon may perform twelve to fourteen surgeries in a single day. On those days, Tom covers the phones and handles patient visits while she is in the operating room. However, when an animal requires bone surgery Sharon administers the anesthesia and Tom handles the operation. Even the clinic's record-keeping is shared, with Tom entering the daily transactions into their computer while Sharon keeps the books.

The Doses nonspecialized work pattern has evolved as a result of their formal training and also out of their strong commitment to service and a well-defined philosophy regarding the care they provide for their patients. Tom explains the rationale behind their decision to run the clinic without assistants or office staff.

We feel if somebody has to wait five minutes in our clinic there's a big problem. Five minutes is just too long. Our customers come in the front door, I wave to them through the window and say, "Be with you in a minute." Then, when I'm finished with the patient I'm seeing, I open the door, let one out and the next one in.

I do everything that has to be done. I ask all the questions, fill out the records, give the vaccines, treat the illness, or check the animal into the hospital. I write up the bill right there and they pay me directly. If they've got a beef about the bill, they don't have to deal with another person, I'll deal with it on the spot. And that's the way Sharon works, too. When a customer calls on the phone, one of us will be on the other end to answer their questions. There's no one in the middle, so there's no miscommunication.

Just communicating with the public is a tremendous job—directions for care, medication, what problems to expect, or how to take care of their pet when they get it home. And if you can't communicate clearly, there will be problems. By dealing directly with our clients, ninety percent of the hassles have been eliminated. And working together without employees eliminates seventy-five percent of what's left.

I've been in clinics where they have so many employees on staff, a morning receptionist and an afternoon receptionist, the technicians, kennel helpers, and doctors, and all these people can't even communicate with each other, much less to their clients. Basically, this business is us, nothing else. And it's not one of us—it's both of us.

Everything about the Doses' clinic has been designed and structured around their philosophy and nonspecialized working style. Even the examining-room partitions, which don't go all the way to the ceiling, facilitate communication between the doctors. While Sharon vaccinates a cat or dog, she can listen to Tom's comments as he treats another animal in the next examination room. If that animal is seen on a subsequent visit by Sharon, she will be able to recall Tom's verbal exchange and the course of treatment. She will be fully knowledgeable, ready to proceed with the examination and appropriate follow-up.

To the rear of the clinic, behind the examination and operating rooms, the two doctors have a small area for relaxation and bookkeeping. This is where they can be found, with their Doberman Pinscher, Murphy, on evenings and weekends, doing paperwork or relaxing, watching television or eating a TV dinner from their microwave—always within earshot of any animal in their kennel.

Sharon and Tom's involvement in their profession and the care of their animal patients is total. Even Murphy plays an important role in their clinic, acting in emergencies as their universal blood donor. The Doses live within walking distance of their clinic and often walk arm-in-arm to and from work. However, the close proximity of their apartment hardly matters since they are rarely home during waking hours—twelve to fourteen hours a day Drs. Sharon and Tom Dose can be found providing the best care possible to the patients of Kings Road Pet Hospital.

IT'S NOT HIS OR HERS—IT'S THEIRS

Clif and Beth Moore are just one of the many couples we met who perform identical functions in their business. The Moores work together as photographers and owners of C & B Moore Photography, operating out of Overton, Nevada. For twelve years they have traveled throughout fourteen western states, following the rodeo circuit in their thirty-two-foot fifth-wheel trailer, their combination home and color photo laboratory. During that time Clif and Beth have covered over twenty thousand miles each year, taking action photographs of rodeo performers in the arena.

Those who participate in sports do so either for the love of the sport or for the love of money, and as Clif points out, "there isn't that much money involved in most rodeos." Often the only mementos the cowboys would take away—besides their bruises—were action photographs of themselves, masterfully captured in the midst of their competitions by the Moores.

Photographing the events in a rodeo arena can be a tough and dangerous business; as action photographers, Clif and Beth were often close enough to the animals and performers to get knocked over. Two years ago, Clif at sixty-one and Beth at fifty-three retired from the rodeo circuit to devote their full professional time to wildlife photography, animal portraits, trail rides, and wagon trips, as well as some freelance advertising work. But for the Moores, retirement means only a change of pace and locations. Beth, who can't conceive of ever retiring from her profession, expressed her amazement at those who don't find pleasure in their work.

We are hard-put to understand those people who work and hate it. But they're afraid to quit. They're afraid to try anything else. We're not. We both like to travel and we both enjoy what we're doing. We enjoy wildlife and bird watching. And if we don't like what we're doing, we'll move on. Life's too short. We might do something else, but we would definitely do it together.

We were intrigued to learn that, as in our own case, the Moores are often asked, "Which of you took this photograph?" and Clif's reply, so similar to ours, is always, "It isn't *mine*, it isn't *hers*, it's *ours*." He elaborated on how they worked together when they were photographing in the rodeo arenas.

We would work two different angles. One of us would take one side and one the other, depending on where the sun was, or where the best shots were possible. We were right in there with the action, both of us shooting the same events. And half the time, we didn't know who took a particular shot. At the end of the day, all the film would be developed together, and it was really never important to us to know who took this or that shot, because it's all *our* work.

Even when the Moores work together in their mobile film lab—a nine-foot darkroom at the rear of their trailer equipped for complete color film processing—they approach the tasks as interchangeable partners. The only area of specialization in either their work or personal lives comes as a result of Beth's sharper eyesight. Clif works the wet, or chemical, side of the lab and Beth the dry side where the photo enlargements are made. All other tasks and responsibilities are shared equally and interchangeably. They work together repairing their truck and doing carpentry on their trailer, and they share all the house-work. Even the bookkeeping is a responsibility they both assume.

The Moores, who were married in 1950, just one week after Beth's graduation from high school, have worked together throughout their marriage, as ranchers in Nevada and Alaska and as freelance rodeo and wildlife photographers. Beth began her photographic career while they were still in Alaska in the late fifties, and Cliff joined her in that profession after they sold their ranch.

When they settled on the idea of rodeo photography, the business took off. Like Sharon and Tom Dose, the Moores chose to work by themselves, without relying on office staff or laboratory assistants. As Beth observes,

> You know, we could've gotten bigger. Everybody said, "Do this...," or "Do that...." but we wanted to work with just the two of us, without extra help around. Besides, we can make enough mistakes ourselves without worrying about somebody else's. Some people just have to get bigger—they need more. We don't have a lot of material things that we need. And it's worked out great with just the two of us.

The Moores are a couple who have maximized their life together, while minimizing and simplifying the material trappings that tie so many of us down to jobs we would rather not be in and places we would like to leave. For these copreneurs, their partnership and nonspecialized working style is based on absolute equality and acceptance of the other's abilities. Clif and Beth can't imagine working in any other way.

BLENDING THE LINES BETWEEN SPECIALIZED SKILLS

Another creative team has found that after years of working together they are gradually merging from a strictly specialized to a less specialized pattern of working. Audrey and Don Wood, who reside in Santa Barbara, California, are award-winning authors and illustrators of children's books, and have created twenty books between them.

Since the fourth grade, Audrey's ambition was to become a children's book author and illustrator. As the eldest of three sisters, she naturally assumed the role of story-teller. Her recollections of those sessions with her sisters as her audience are idyllic. Her mother, however, still recalls her youngest daughter crying in alarm, "Mommy! Mommy! Audrey's making the snakes crawl off the page again!" Audrey was spinning one of her vivid tales, using *The Illustrated Wildlife Encyclopedia* as a visual aid.

Don's father was a self-made man who worked his way from picking grapes to owing his own farm in California's Central Valley, growing oranges, peaches, apricots, almonds and sweet potatoes. Don's brother, who is twenty-five years his senior, took over the ranch and turned it into an enormous success. Although Don remembers always being surrounded by strong and successful adults, there was no one in his young life who supported his artistic ambitions.

> I decided in the fifth or sixth grade to be an artist. I really have no idea where it came from. My family discouraged the idea and tried to get me to do anything else in the world. And although I was a nice tractable kid and did everything else they wanted, by God, I was going to be an artist!
>
> It interests me where that strength and decisiveness and vision came from because I can think of nothing in the family that would have created it in me. And in that little tiny farming community, out in the middle of nowhere, here I was determined to become an artist. Audrey had been surrounded with art all her life, her father and grandfather were artists—but there wasn't an artist within a hundred miles of me when I was growing up.

Don and Audrey met in Berkeley, California, where Don was a student at the California College of Arts and Crafts. Audrey, who had just arrived from Little Rock, Arkansas, had seen Don's work and wanted to meet the artist. The attraction they felt for each other's artistic talents drew the couple together into a close friendship that developed into their continuing love affair.

Many people say that it's difficult for a couple to work together in a business, and we have often heard that to work together as artists would be impossible. Don and Audrey Wood have proven both those assumptions false. Their combined talents have won them many honors, including a Caldecott Honor Book Award, an American Library Association Notable Children's Book Award, a Parent's Choice Book Award, and the distinction of one of their titles having been selected as one of the *New York Times* Ten Best Illustrated Children's Books of the year.

When they began their collaboration, distinct divisions of creative responsibility structured their working relationship— Audrey was the author and Don the illustrator. Their successful publishing career together was launched when Audrey, a fourth-generation artist, began writing and illustrating children's books for publishers in the United States. She had already established a reputation as a writer and illustrator of children's books in England, where she had been published for many years prior to the couple's collaborations. Over time, on various publishing projects, the lines of specialized creativity between Audrey's words and Don's art have occasionally disappeared. The couple have now coauthored as well as coillustrated some of their books.

The Wood's first collaboration was *Moonflute*, published in 1980, written by Audrey and illustrated by Don. This sentimental and romantic book has become a classic that is cherished by children and adults alike. And Don's original oil paintings for this beautiful book were displayed at the Metropolitan Museum of Art. Ironically, Audrey had submitted this title to thirty publishers before it was accepted for publication. It has since become a best-seller.

We met with the couple in their Victorian home and sat in their cozy living room, surrounded by the life-sized fantasy characters that Audrey had fashioned out of papier-mâché, which served as models for characters in the Wood's new book, *Elbert's Bad Word*. Audrey and Don filled us in on how their working partnership began. Before her manuscript for *Moonflute* was accepted for publication, Audrey had realized that the artwork necessary for this story was not suitable to her artistic style. After receiving numerous illustrator's samples, she persuaded Don to submit his work to her publisher. "They liked it, and called us within three days," Audrey remembers. "That's where it began, and we've been doing one book together each year ever since."

In both their personal and working lives, Audrey and Don have created a supportive environment that includes a mutual understanding of the unique realms in which they each work. The emotional and intellectual rapport that exists between them has resulted in a secure environment, one in which risk, growth, and supportive criticism thrive.

Increasingly, the Woods are encouraging one another to move toward a more nonspecialized working style, one in which Audrey urges Don to write and Don supports Audrey's continuing artistic development. While Audrey's artistic style is naturally spontaneous, loose, and expressionistic, Don's is much more controlled and illusionistic as a result of his formal training. Before their artistic collaboration on *Elbert's Bad Word*, a delightful tale that Audrey wrote and the couple coillustrated, Don remembers how he first began enhancing Audrey's artwork.

Audrey is a compulsive doodler, and loves to doodle while talking on the phone. I would come to the telephone and find her fascinating drawings all around. I love to shade things, making them round. I love the illusion of roundness and would take her flat little doodles, shade them, and give them form and dimension. I began to enjoy this a lot and found myself searching out her drawings just so I could shade them. I thought her drawings were pure genius, and yet the shading is something she wasn't very much at home with.

When Audrey wrote *Elbert's Bad Word* and furnished the drawings for it, we were struck with the opportunity to collaborate artistically. Audrey and I took some of the strengths of her work, the wonderful wacky way she draws humans and the strange perspectives—all that fanciful style that my formal training knocked out of me—and added my skills as a colorist and shader to complement her artistic spontaneity.

I couldn't have created a world like that alone, but it's wonderful, magnificent, charming, and offbeat. And alone Audrey would have been incapable of producing that style of art, which was the result of our collaboration. Together, a *third* artist emerged between us. This is a perfect example of us complementing each other and working together to produce something that neither one of us could have produced by ourselves. And from that collaboration we are learning from each other—Audrey is picking up artistic techniques from me, and her art is growing, while my art is also evolving as a result of the way we've learned to share how we work.

The Woods are gradually moving into a less specialized work pattern. They will no doubt continue to work together on books while maintaining their separate functions as wordsmith and artist. However, they are increasingly encouraging one another to expand their individual realms of involvement, allowing their collaborations to blend their various artistic talents and creativity together.

SHARING ROLES OUT ON THE TRAIL

In our search for couples, we stumbled on a bonanza of copreneurs, all working together, at Gold Canyon Stables in Apache Junction, Arizona. Nestled at the foot of the Superstition Mountains, Gold Canyon is the home of a unique group of couples whose love for horses and the outdoors has drawn them together in a blend of enterprises as well as friendships. Depending on the season, visitors to the stables will find these couples helping one another in their enterprises and assuring that each trail ride is a memorable one for the stable's guests.

At the heart of this group are Don and Shelley Donnelly, owners and operators of the stables. During the winter months the Donnellys are joined by old friends: a husband and wife who are rodeo performers, and famous for their team of trained sheep; and a second couple who run the boot shop located at the stables where customers can purchase handmade boots and saddles. Year-round, a third couple is responsible for catering all the rides. When these old friends are not working, they often can be found riding the range together, enjoying each other's company, the horses, and their mutual love of the wilderness.

Don is a colorful six-foot-six cowboy who is never without a pinch of chewing tobacco in his cheek and his ten gallon hat pushed back on his forehead—a true character out of the Old West. Shelley is an attractive modern cowgirl and the perfect foil for Don's rugged individualism and western humor.

Don has worked with horses for twenty-five years, and he and Shelley have worked together since their marriage in 1969. In 1982 the Donnellys opened Gold Canyon Stables. Running a

stable with a hundred head of horses and a crew of wranglers is
a physically grueling and demanding enterprise. The hours are
long, often beginning as early as three or four in the morning
and continuing on until long after dark. Displaying his wry
sense of humor, Don quips, "We work seven days a week,
three-hundred sixty-four and a half days a year—we're closed
half a day for Christmas, so ya see, we're not really full time."

In a business centered around animals there can be no days
off, and Don and Shelley work hard to maintain the prime
condition of their stock. Don nearly bursts with pride describing his horses.

> I'm real proud of 'em. They're big and stout, they're full of grain and
> ready to ride. They eat the best hay money can buy, and we buy lots
> of grain for 'em, too. You can just tell they feel good all the time,
> 'cause when we turn 'em out in the pen, they'll buck and kick and
> run—and that's after a hard day's work.

A good portion of Don and Shelley's business is providing
horses and tour guides for pack trips into such rugged areas as
the Superstition Mountains, Monument Valley, the Grand Canyon, and other wilderness territory throughout Arizona, much
of which is accessible only on horseback. Often, the horses must
be transported great distances by truck to the trailhead. The
number of pack trips they lead sometimes requires that the
Donnellys split up, each heading a separate group, or one
staying behind to run things at headquarters. At the stables or
on the trail, Don and Shelley are interchangeable in many tasks.
As Don says,

> Shelley can do anything I can. We have tractors, trucks, big rigs,
> and stock trailers. We'll transport from twenty to thirty head of
> horses for each one of our rides anywhere in the state. And if you
> need that load of horses somewhere, don't wait for me 'cause
> Shelley can haul 'em to ya. She takes the big rigs just like I do. She
> might do it a little different, but you get the same results.

Much of Don and Shelley's work revolves around the telephone. Each year, over sixteen thousand customers come to
Gold Canyon Stables. And many of those riders have to be

convinced over the telephone that a day in the saddle is for them. Horseback riding is a leisure-time activity, which the Donnellys know all too well is a real luxury. Competing against the horses for that leisure time are literally hundreds of other activities from which their customers can choose—television, movies, golf, or simply relaxing around the pool at the nearby resort. Their clients are looking for a memorable experience, one they can go home and tell their friends about, and Don and Shelley have to do a lot of selling to convince potential customers that what they want can be found at Gold Canyon Stables. Therefore when Don and Shelley are not working with the horses, or out on the trail, they can be found on the phone, answering questions, talking to individuals or resorts, making them aware of what the stables have to offer. Don explained,

> If they're shopping on the phone, you've only got one shot at 'em. And if what they hear is good, if they think you're interested and know what you're doing, that's your opportunity to get 'em here.
>
> I've got to sell—I mean literally sell every horseback ride. It's not like food. Here we're dealing with something that people dang sure don't need. They sure don't need to ride a horse. And the next thing is—they don't want to. I'm just scared enough by that to think I've got to be here. I've got to answer the phone, I've got to sell, and I've got to make sure they hear what they want to hear. The telephone is the best selling tool we've got.

After we had spent two days at the stables, listening to many colorful phone calls, it was clear that Don has mastered the art of low-key telephone sales. Even if it's a wrong number, he can charm a caller into coming out and "giving it a try." We sat in the small office that Don and Shelley share, listening to him spin his charm on the telephone, stopping between sentences to spit tobacco into his spittoon.

> This is Gold Canyon.
> Have you ever been here? You called the wrong place, didn't you?
> Well, wait a minute now. Will you do something for me? Go ahead and keep your reservation at that other place, okay?
> Now ya say you're in charge of the whole group? Well, Sandy, they're gonna depend on you to have something real nice. And if it

isn't real good, they're gonna be after you, aren't they? Holy cow. Whooee!—you got troubles then! Before this happens, come on out and see us for just a minute and let us show you what you're gonna miss. Before you decide for sure, we'll take you out to the gold mine where we set up the Sunday breakfasts and put on the barbecues. I'd like to show you what this place is really like. I think you'll be real impressed.

Well, thank ya Sandy.

Don hung up the receiver and turned to us, saying, "She called the wrong place, but we got her anyway. If she'll come out, it's eighty-five percent in our favor."

Like many of their copreneurial counterparts, the Donnellys have accepted many areas of individual responsibility. Shelley maintains the books and travels into town for supplies, and Don handles most of the business contacts, insurance, and equipment purchases. However, there are more areas that are shared between them than not. Shelley works the phone just as hard as Don, and with an equal amount of her own western charm. In addition to their joint marketing efforts, on any day she and Don can both be found saddling horses, hitching a team up to one of the large hay wagons, leading a group of riders back into the Superstition Mountains, or driving one of the rigs loaded with horses to some remote trailhead.

The operation at Gold Canyon was one of the larger and more complex enterprises we uncovered in which both partners continue to share so many responsibilities and tasks equally, working interchangeably rather than collaboratively, in a nonspecialized work style.

The couples we've just met have all settled into nonspecialized working patterns. Some work collaboratively together, while others have found that working interchangeably, performing the same tasks, works best for them. All of the enterprises we have discussed here, except for Gold Canyon Stables, are run with only the two partners or a relatively small staff. But while these businesses may be small when measured by the number of employees, that does not mean they aren't capable of making a bundle of money.

6

When Roles and Tasks Are Divided— Specialization

Just as we discovered many copreneurs who have adopted a nonspecialized work style, so did we encounter a number of couples who have staked out distinct areas of specialization within their particular businesses. Those who elect to work in this fashion do so in diverse enterprises, although theirs are usually larger in terms of staff than are the nonspecialized enterprises. We found electrical contractors, auctioneers, manufacturers, food franchisers, square-dance callers, health-care practitioners, and direct-mail catalogers, to mention a few.

Many couples would find working together while sharing functions and responsibilities totally incomprehensible. Some might even suggest that functions and tasks just simply *have* to be divided between the partners if the relationship is to survive. For these couples, specialization may indeed be a prerequisite to success.

The differences in copreneurial work styles did not necessarily come about as a result of the products or services provided by the enterprise, but arose for the most part from the style of working together that was dictated by the partners' individual talents and personal relationship. These coentrepreneurs who

have elected to assume responsibilities separate from their
partner, like those couples who share all tasks and responsibilities, would be hard-pressed to work together in any other
fashion.

DRAWING SEPARATE LINES
OF RESPONSIBILITY

Irene Cohen, of Irene Cohen Personnel Services, expresses
this viewpoint, and describes how and why she and Sy have
structured their separate business functions.

> We have found the only way for us to work together, because we
> both have very strong personalities and are tremendously talented
> people, is to separate our responsibilities. My area is marketing,
> sales, and administration, and Sy's is the financial end.
>
> He has his own group of people in his department that he hires,
> deals with, and takes care of. Sometimes he asks my advice and we
> toss things back and forth, but in his area he makes the ultimate
> decisions. And everything else in the company falls within my
> responsibility. For us, that's the only way we can work together.
> Otherwise, with nearly a hundred employees, everybody would
> report to two bosses, and that just wouldn't work.
>
> We've had disagreements at those times when one of us infringed
> on the other's territory without being asked. It would drive Sy crazy
> if I went into the accounting department and told one of his people,
> "You're doing it the wrong way." I have done that inadvertently and
> Sy very clearly said that I was interfering. And it goes both ways—I
> wouldn't want him in here messing up my work. By drawing those
> lines of responsibilities we have eliminated a lot of difficult
> problems.

The way in which the Cohens work together is most certainly
different from how we collaborate in our advertising agency or
how Tom and Sharon Dose work interchangeably in their veterinary clinic. The Cohens' decision to work independently from
one another arose from their individual strengths and talents as
well as a need to separate responsibilities and spheres of influence in their agency.

IN THE LIMELIGHT
AND BEHIND THE SCENES

Many copreneurs we met who have specialized roles in their business have developed their supportive, yet quite distinct, niches as a result of their unique individual capabilities and talents. One such couple is Donna and Harvey Clar who since 1972 have operated the Harvey Clar Auction Gallery in Oakland, California.

The Clars, who have known each other since 1960, and who have worked together during much of that time, were married in 1972, the same year they opened their auction gallery. Harvey, who was eighteen years old when he began his career, now has over forty years experience as an auctioneer. And Donna has considerable experience in the business as well, having worked with Harvey for several years before their marriage.

To the outsider, auctions are an intriguing mystery. It's a business few people understand because there isn't an auction house on every block. To many of us the fast pace, the glamour, and the dread that we may signal an offer with an inadvertent scratch of the nose is the extent of our knowledge of this complex industry.

The auction itself is the culmination of behind-the-scenes activities that require vast amounts of negotiation, purchases, advance planning, paperwork, and organization. Every thirty days, before their auctions, the Clars oversee a complex cycle of events leading to the preview of the merchandise and the auctions themselves. And at the end of each month's sale a new cycle begins for the Clars and their hard-working staff.

Merchandise finds its way into an auction house through various avenues—consignments from estates, merchants, or individuals, as well as outright purchases by the gallery. Once the merchandise arrives it must be numbered, cataloged, and set up for previewing. The preview itself is an exciting event. Each item, from an antique paperweight to a complete nineteenth-century dining room ensemble is displayed in the gallery to its best advantage. It is not uncommon to see interested buyers arriving at a preview with their own piano tuner, furniture refinisher, or auto mechanic to give their expert opinions concerning particular items.

A complete auction series will feature as many as twenty-five hundred items from forty to fifty consignees. And these goods will end up as the cherished possessions of six or seven hundred individuals.

Following the preview, in preparation for the sale, every item must be moved from the gallery floor and placed behind the auction platform, ready to be brought onto the Clars' revolving stage at just the right moment. Harvey, who describes himself as a "soft-sell auctioneer," auctions one hundred and fifteen to one hundred and twenty items an hour, ranging from nineteenth- and early twentieth-century goods and midmarket art—paintings valued at up to forty thousand dollars—to antique rugs and automobiles; and some of those vintage cars can sell for even more.

Harvey truly loves his job, and that fact comes across to the audience during his lively sales, which are punctuated with jokes and asides by the often irreverent auctioneer. He admits,

> I like to kid around a lot. Not long ago a Persian rug sold for twenty thousand dollars and after the final bid I said, "Sir, that little hole over there on the right side, you're not even going to notice it very much. Just take that table over there and cover it up." And the audience loved it, they get a big kick out of it, and the buyers always take my kidding the right way.

Donna and Harvey perfectly complement one another's considerable abilities, and both acknowledge the indispensable role the other plays in their successful auction house. Because the business carries Harvey's name, he is the more visible partner to the public. Donna comments that at times,

> I have to wear a name tag or people won't know who I am. Unless you're a large corporation, in the auction business the auctioneer's name is going to stand out. But we don't fight over who is first and who is second. We each know what our niches are and we do them well. There is no way I could do what Harvey does, and there is no way he would want to or could do what I do, because our niches are so very different.
>
> Harvey is the sales end of the organization—he's the front man.

He makes his deals and I do the paper work. In fact, there are four of us in the office all doing the unseen work that makes the operation go. This leaves Harvey free to do what he does best.

While Harvey's position as auctioneer places him in the limelight, his behind-the-scenes functions also include appraisals for courts, charities, probate, estates, and insurance as well as appraisals of complete automobile dealerships or other businesses that are changing hands, being refinanced, or going on the auction block. Harvey describes how their business responsibilities fall into distinct areas.

What I do is the buying, the selling, and that end of the business. And what Donna does is all the financial details of each auction that are so necessary when tying up all those loose ends resulting from the large number of sales. She cleans it all up, puts it all together, makes sure checks go out and that the buys are paid for. She also makes sure items get checked in correctly. All that work gets done on her end and I certainly don't put my nose in there.

I couldn't run the business without having somebody in the office taking care of it. If there is a weak point, I sure have it—and the office work is it. I'm not good at details and Donna is a perfect detailer. So we complement each other.

If both of us were auctioneers, with a team running the office under us, I could see that being a problem. I'm not saying it wouldn't work, but because both of our egos would be going all the time, there might be competition and problems. As it is, there's no competition between us because we're working together for the same thing—we're on the same team.

I'll support Donna in anything that has to do with the office, or bookkeeping or finances. And I don't have to worry about investments or overhead because Donna takes care of all that, both in the business and at home. I defer to her one hundred percent. I won't even get into it. I'd just say, "Hey, that's her bone." We had two guys come in the other day from credit card companies and they were expecting to talk to me. I told them, "You don't want to talk to me—that's not my ballpark at all. You want to talk to Donna, that's her area and I don't get into it."

While Harvey may appear from the outside to be the dominant partner, the Clars are, in fact, remarkably equal. Much of their work requires travel to appraise collections, estates, and businesses, and during these appraisals Donna and Harvey often work together as a team.

Many of their clients bring goods to auction as a result of a life-altering event—a move to a retirement community or smaller home, and quite often because of the death of a loved one. The items being auctioned have deep sentimental value, and the Clars' clients often have difficulty seeing their possessions go under the gavel. In these instances, both Donna and Harvey will spend considerable time to put the client at ease. They recognize the emotions and ties that each item can represent. Harvey observes,

> I think a lot of people do business with us because of the attention and understanding that we express for their situation and for the items they are letting go. When they call us, they're dealing with just me and Donna and they feel good about that. We discuss their inventory and tell them what we can do for them. We explain how our crew will come in and carefully pack every item, and we let them know that Donna and I will be there as well.
>
> When they call other auction houses, and a kid comes out to see them, they're very unhappy. Often a young appraiser doesn't have that sense of warmth that we express. He looks at every item as just an item, rather than as a piece of the people themselves. He'll come in and say, "Oh yeah, that'll bring about seventy-five dollars."
>
> I'll look at that same item and say, "That's just a beautiful piece," or "It's hard to put a price on a piece like that when it has so much personal history behind it." Sometimes when you're there, they like you to be with them emotionally. And when Donna and I go together, people really appreciate that. Often, Donna and I will spend a whole morning with a client, they'll make lunch for us, Donna will walk through their gardens, and together we'll put them at ease.

While Harvey Clar Auction Gallery is indeed a success and its reputation extends throughout California, and increasingly throughout the country, it is still a very personal enterprise, one in which the personality of both owners continues to play a significant role. The Clars have carved out a comfortable niche within their industry, while maintaining a healthy growth of between fifteen and twenty percent each year.

When Donna and Harvey first opened their gallery, they were warned that it would take ten years and one hundred thousand dollars to build it into a successful enterprise. Looking back, Donna states with understandable pride and a sense of accomplishment, "At the time, we didn't have ten years or that kind of money. But the advice was sound, it did take that long, but instead of a hundred thousand dollars, it took three hundred and fifty thousand—and a lot of hard work and dedication. But we're still here, and we're a success."

Not only do the Clars recognize what they each do best, they also have a clear vision of what their business does best—and that is not to try to emulate Christie's or Sotheby's. Their gallery, which is today a multimillion dollar business, was not an overnight success. "In the first couple of years," Harvey admits, "if the telephone rang, it was either my ex-wife or my mother." Their success was the result of a specialized area of expertise and merchandise and a tenacious dedication to providing a unique service.

PUTTING THEIR DIFFERENCES TO WORK

Claude and Donna Jeanloz of The Renovator's Supply, headquartered in Millers Falls, Massachusetts, have put their distinctly different personalities and skills to work creating a highly successful enterprise. The Jeanlozes were married twenty years ago in West Africa, where Claude was serving in the Peace Corps. At the end of his tour, the couple settled in New England where they began renovating their two-hundred-year-old Massachusetts farm house. During that process, Claude and Donna discovered that authentic replacement fixtures were extremely difficult to come by.

With the profits from a second home they had restored in Quebec, Claude and Donna launched their direct-mail venture from the kitchen table in their Millers Falls home. That first catalog consisted of about three hundred products for home renovation that the couple had identified as difficult to locate. Using the *Thomas Register* to find the manufacturers of those products, the Jeanlozes ordered three of each item, photographed them in their backyard, set the copy on their typewriter, and mailed fifty thousand black-and-white catalogs during their first year of business.

Today, their diverse operation is unquestionably the largest employer in the small New England community of Millers Falls. The Renovator's Supply manufactures over seventy percent of the items contained in their two catalogs; publishes a quarterly magazine; and operates ten retail outlets located in the Northeast and reaching as far south as Baltimore. The Renovator's Old Mill, the company headquarters and manufacturing facility, is an historic complex of buildings dating back to 1870 that covers a quarter of a million square feet on forty acres of land.

Following a tour of their enormous facility, we rested comfortably during the evening in the couple's warm and spacious home, listening to their story. Claude observed,

> Right from day one, we had distinct areas of responsibility. I took the photographs and Donna wrote the copy. In the beginning we used to bet how many orders there would be in the mailbox. Donna was always under by fifty percent, and I'd usually be over fifteen to twenty percent. Those were the days when we were getting fifteen to twenty orders a day. Today orders come in at a daily rate of between a thousand and fifteen hundred.
>
> Our mailbox bets highlight one of our major differences. Donna dreads getting the mail—there might be something bad in it. And I bound out to the mailbox because of all the good stuff that's waiting. Donna has always acted as a leveler and a brake, while I'm the idea and action person. I feel I've got the strength, determination and drive to do something, and Donna's got the brains.

Because of the tremendous diversity of their enterprise—the direct mail operation, the huge manufacturing facility, the retail stores, and the publishing of their magazine, *Victorian Homes*, Donna sees her function as "the brakes" as being entirely necessary. "Otherwise, God knows what we'd be into. Not only do I think about the negative things, but the positive things as well—its a balancing act."

While we were visiting the Jeanlozes, Claude was immersed in the operation of their new bindery equipment, recently installed in their manufacturing facility. Donna explained to us the importance of this addition to their already complex operation,

> Since our catalog comes out every six weeks, it's very important that it be mailed out on an even schedule. Over this past winter we bought a bindery line and are now binding our own catalogs. What had been happening, typically, was that our printer would dump over a million catalogs into the mail within a three-day period. The result was that we would be swamped with orders for the first three weeks and dry for the next three.
>
> Binding the catalogs ourselves is enabling us to mail at a steady rate of fifty thousand catalogs each day, and our responses are also now coming in at a steady rate that affects our whole operation positively—customer service, shipping, stocking, and manufacturing. Our new bindery allows us to even everything out.

The Jeanlozes have clearly divided areas of responsibility. In addition to publishing *Victorian Homes*, which was launched in 1981 and now has a circulation of seventy thousand, Donna is involved with the retail stores and handles all those aspects of the corporation dealing with legal issues, copyright infringements, patents, and trademarks—all the things that are so necessary when an organization reaches the size of The Renovator's Supply.

Claude views his responsibilities as being twofold. The first is in the area of corporate asset management, to develop and protect the assets of the company and to maximize the future benefits of those assets. His second area of involvement is running the manufacturing operation of their company's three-thousand products and making all the decisions in manufacturing regarding new processes and new products. The day-to-day running of their direct-mail operation is handled by Cindy Harris, the president of the company.

For the eight weeks before our visit, Claude's intense involvement in the catalog bindery line had necessitated Donna's handling of any crises that arose, even in areas normally outside her expertise. Donna explained,

During this and other times when Claude has his nose to the grindstone, I can always find somebody over here who knows how to deal with a problem if I don't. Fortunately, we're at a point in the organization where that works very well. I can find someone, whether it's the head of maintenance or Cindy Harris. Somebody else can do it if Claude or I can't.

Even though Claude and Donna own equal shares in their corporation and profit-share equally, Donna makes no pretense about who runs their company.

He's not the president of the company, but he runs the business and every one of our employees knows that. He's the top of the organizational umbrella. But there are instances in which I am more powerful—personnel matters, for example. He'll express his opinion, but then say, "You take care of it." And at that, I do what I think is right.

In the case of our magazine, I'm the publisher and he hasn't got the foggiest notion of what's going on because it's really not necessary for him to know. It's profitable and it's under control, and he leaves well enough alone—which I think is a terrific way to operate. Likewise, with mail order, he keeps track of what happens in that area but as long as Cindy has her act together and things run smoothly, he doesn't mess in her affairs either.

Claude and Donna's highly specialized style of working together allows them to oversee a multifaceted and growing organization. The seeds of thought that first germinated in 1978, when the couple saw a window of opportunity in the direct-mail business, have grown and blossomed. And for the past decade, the Jeanlozes have continued to inform ever-increasing numbers of renovation enthusiasts of their company's tradition of quality products that are available at a reasonable price through their catalogs and stores.

A NEW FACE IN THE FAMILY BUSINESS

The name Christine Valmy is synonymous with skin care in the United States. In 1961 Madame Valmy arrived in this country from her native Romania with only $15 in her pocket, and her young daughter and parents to support. Since 1965, when she opened her first salon, she has established a reputation throughout the world for her modern scientific approach to skin care, her genius for formulation, and her high-quality skin-care products.

In 1971 Madame Valmy was recognized by the Ninety-Second Congress of the United States for her outstanding contributions to education in America through the creation of the first school for skin-care specialists. Over twenty thousand skin-care specialists have graduated from her schools, creating a new branch in the beauty industry, known as "Esthetics."

Marina, Christine's daughter, was educated in Europe and returned to this country in 1968 at the age of seventeen. "It was a difficult period of adjustment," Marina remembers. The hippie generation was in full bloom and she found herself in a state of culture shock.

> I had been raised very strictly abroad and the adjustment was really quite difficult for me. Coming to the university here I felt so different from everyone else—I spoke a different language, and culturally it was a different period. Everyone was without makeup, with their hair hanging down, wearing jeans, and I had always dressed more formally. I've always worn my nails red, but in America nobody had red nails at that time.

Because of her loneliness and insecurities in a strange country, Marina found herself attracted for the wrong reasons to the wrong man, one of her college professors, whom she married shortly after graduation. During that unsuccessful eight-and-a-half year relationship Marina, who had joined her mother's firm, was devoting all of her emotional energies to her career in a desperate effort to block out the unhappiness of her personal life.

> Every day, seven days a week, I would come into the office because I had nothing to do at home. I never wanted to accept the fact that I had made a mistake—not even to my mother. People who knew me then and know me now, they don't recognize me. I used to be very

stern looking, I never smiled. I always wore black or navy blue
because that's what he wanted me to wear, and I was very unhappy.

Following her divorce, Marina met Peter de Haydu when they
were introduced by his mother. For Marina, it was like stepping
out of a black-and-white film into full Technicolor. Within seven
days of their first date Peter had proposed, and they were
married six months later.

Marina and Peter moved to his native Venezuela where he
headed seventeen South American companies as a CEO for the
Alcoa affiliate company. Although ecstatically happy in her new
marriage with Peter, living in Venezuela was another cultural
shock for Marina.

We moved to Venezuela because Peter thought we were going to
remain there forever. He had a very, very good position in the
company and was being groomed by the existing chairman to be
the next person to take over the holding company. But in Venezuela
I was just a housewife. In New York I'd been working in my
company and had all sorts of people I could call upon—my staff,
my secretary. But in Venezuela, I couldn't even go out shopping
alone because of the politics. It was a real shock for me.

In 1986, Peter and Marina returned to the United States to be
with Peter's mother, who was critically ill. Peter recalls,

We came up because my mother's doctor told me she had only
several months to go. I had to make a decision whether I was going
to go back to Wall Street, go to a major firm, or make a big
departure from what I'd been doing. Marina's mother had been
trying to convince me for some time to come into the family
business. She believed that my background in international finance
and investment banking would be invaluable for the firm. Prior to
my position in Venezuela, I had worked for Dillon, Read, a bou-
tique investment bank on Wall Street, and for British Petroleum in
their London marketing headquarters. My mother-in-law also
wanted me to join the business because she and her husband were
getting to the age where they wanted to retire. And, of course, she
wanted her daughter back in New York.

It was a tough decision. I had to consider how this move would
be viewed in the industry. I didn't feel there would be any bias

toward a man leading a cosmetics company, but I did have some concern that there might be bias against someone who is the son-in-law of the company founder. However, after much deliberation, I decided to take the plunge and made a commitment to the firm. We've been involved in the family enterprise now for the past two and a half years.

Peter's decision to join the firm with the couple dividing the shares of the corporation on a fifty-fifty basis was a management stroke of genius. Marina acknowledged that neither her talents nor those of her mother were in the realm of business management.

The business had remained more or less at a plateau for the past six or seven years. We had grown in spite of ourselves, not because of ourselves, and now had over a hundred and sixty employees. My strengths are in retail, I am very good with clients and know how to run the salons. And my mother is the most creative person—she's a genius at product formulation. Yesterday she went into the lab and made a new masque in about fifteen minutes that she had developed twenty-five years ago and yet she had not had the formula. She just whipped it out and sent it to *Harper's Bazaar* immediately. She can just open a jar, smell it, look at the texture and tell you its chemical ingredients.

But she would be the first to admit that she is completely non-commercial. When it comes to marketing and doing business my mother is her own worst enemy. We had never had someone who came into our firm saying, "Okay, you need this plan, and this is how you should go about achieving this objective," or "This is how you should structure your franchises." Before Peter joined the company we were a Mom and Pop operation, just because we didn't have a background in business. And while my step-father is a very successful businessman in Europe, doing business there is very different from doing business in the United States.

Peter saw the potential at Christine Valmy. Americans are awakening to the importance of skin care, not just as a passing fad but as an important part of a health care regime. Christine Valmy already had an infrastructure—it had the products, the schools, the experience of running salons, and the manufacturing equipment, as well as one of the most respected names in the industry. For Peter, it was merely a matter of putting the right business plan and marketing formula into action.

Since Peter and Marina have assumed full responsibility for the operation of Christine Valmy, the company has made incredible strides. And education has been an important thrust of the couple's growth plan. Beauty salons in the United States focus on hair care, which is much less scientific than skin care. "It's not like shampoo or conditioner," Peter explained. "You simply cannot walk into a drug store or a department store and pick it up."

Rigorous training is required for skin-care professionals, who in turn educate their clients to the importance and value of the product. In twelve months during 1987 and 1988, Christine Valmy opened two new schools, one in New York and one in New Jersey. In addition, the couple are proud that the largest beauty company in Japan, Takigawa & Co., Ltd., has selected Christine Valmy as the skin-care product they will introduce into that country. That Japanese firm is backing its commitment with a huge salon in the Ginza area and two schools that have already trained twenty-five skin-care professionals.

To run a multinational operation that includes salons, franchising, schools, product development, and manufacturing requires diversified talents and individual concentrations of effort, and Peter and Marina have divided the tasks along the lines of their individual interests, expertise, and talents.

Because of Marina's people skills and strong knowledge of their product and retail operations, she has assumed responsibility for the management of their salons and franchises in this country and abroad. Marina also oversees the development of their schools, and during construction she acts as a general contractor, laying out the facility and buying all materials. Advertising, publicity, and the image of the company are also her areas of responsibility, and are all handled out of her Fifth Avenue office in New York City.

Peter, operating out of the company's corporate headquarters in Pine Brook, New Jersey, is very much the business end of the organization—financial, marketing, and operations, including the overall management of the manufacturing and educational facilities. Madame Valmy remains the firm's goodwill ambassador, dealing with public relations and continuing her work in current product development, although these days she is playing a less active role in the company. Peter predicts,

> Over the long term I see the whole operation as coming together and becoming one. I would like to see Marina eventually phase out her activities in the retail side and concentrate in other areas such as product development—things she is really strong at, instead of running around trying to sort out personnel problems. That's such a waste of her talents and abilities.
>
> Our company has contributed immensely to the awareness of skin care in this country, and we believe we are going to be very successful. Because when people really understand the way skin works and how to care for it properly, they will have an understanding for our product and what we have been doing for the past twenty-five years and will continue doing in the future.

Peter and Marina's involvement in their company represents the only venture we investigated that the copreneurs themselves did not originate. It remains to be seen whether Christine Valmy will evolve into a true family business, as opposed to a copreneurial enterprise.

Family businesses are not necessarily run by couples who are in twenty-four hour relationships. Often they are the enterprise of siblings, fathers and sons, or other relatives working together. As such, they do not always enjoy the trust, communication, freedom from competition, clearly shared objectives, and level of commitment that are characteristic of all of the successful entrepreneurial couples we met. All of these elements we found to be firmly established and actively operating in Peter and Marina's working and personal relationships.

Copreneurs who have elected to divide their tasks and responsibilities by specializing have chosen to work together with their partners in a fashion that capitalizes on their individual strengths, skills, and areas of interest. Whether a couple decide to work side by side, sharing the same or different tasks, or to work separately, sometimes in different offices and occasionally in separate facilities, their respective areas of responsibility

always represent meaningful portions of their enterprise. We
found that when these couples work in circumstances that
separate them physically, the contact and communications between them remain at a remarkably high level. Many couples
schedule the noon hour as a time to meet, to discuss the
morning's events and to enjoy their lunches together.

Because the Clars often work through the weekends, Donna
balances her heavy work load by taking one day a week off. But
on that day out of the office she still drives into town to meet
Harvey for lunch. When businesses require one partner to travel
away from home, every couple we met stressed that not a day
goes by without at least one telephone call to their partner—
from wherever they are in the world—to check on the office, and
just to say "I love you." As Marina notes,

> Even though Peter works out of our New Jersey headquarters, if
> something important occurs, we're on the telephone saying, "Hey,
> something great just happened!" Peter will call me a couple of
> times a day when he has a few moments, or if one of us is feeling
> down, the other will call and say, "You know what? I love you."
> And that's nice.

Whether copreneurs elect to work in a specialized or nonspecialized style, they do so in a fashion that is always noncompetitive and supportive of their partner's areas of responsibility.
Their shared goals and lack of interpersonal competition are a
result of their ability to communicate freely and not to put
themselves above their partner or their enterprise.

CHAPTER

7

Turn Your Egos Into Wegos

S trong individual egos can get in the way of good management. When there are two intimate partners in a copreneurial enterprise, each with a strong ego, there is a need to arrive at a balance. We do not suggest that the partners place their egos on hold, or learn to rein them in. Rather we believe that strong egos are necessary in any entrepreneurial venture and that two egos blended into one *wego*—a combined ego shared noncompetitively by the partners and directed constructively outside their relationship—can be a powerful combination of forces.

The blending of two distinct egos can't be expected to occur overnight. But once blended, the resulting wego is very different from the individual egos from which it evolved. And one by-product of this blending of egos is the demise of self-centered competition between partners.

The ego, that independent self so central to western thought, mirrors the capitalist ethic of competitive individualism. And while egos often result in competitive isolation, serving those objectives that lead to mastery and control based on win-lose premises, wegos are nonauthoritarian, pluralistic, and grounded on humanistic values of interrelating based on win-win assumptions.

At the center of the ego is "I, myself—Number One." A fully developed wego, on the other hand, focuses on "we, ourselves," placing the emphasis on the relationship and the enterprise rather than on the individual. A wego evolves with the realization that both partners are contributing one hundred percent to their venture. It comes with the pride of knowing that together you've accomplished your goal—not with the statement "I'm proud of it because *I* did it," but rather "I'm proud of it because *we* did it." Wegos evolve out of the self-confidence of each partner knowing that together they possess the individual capabilities to achieve their goals and the realization that without *ourselves*, the concept of *myself* is meaningless.

For couples who allow their egos to merge, there exists the possibility of new kinds of management and leadership that result from a holistic approach of relating between themselves and those outside their relationship.

When Drs. Sharon and Tom Dose opened their veterinary clinic in Reno they felt, like other professionals, the need to have their *own* clients. Tom remembers, "I didn't want them going to somebody else because they were *my* clients, and that's an ego thing." For their first few months in business they would measure their customer index cards with a little centimeter ruler and "guesstimate" the size of their growing clientele at forty records per centimeter. But for the past few years, Sharon and Tom haven't bothered to count because they are confident of the success of their venture. As Sharon observes,

> We lost our ego. Veterinarians, doctors, and dentists have a great deal of ego investment in the number of clients they can claim for their practice. But we don't *own* any clients—if they come through our door, then they're our clients. We'll help them, we'll help anybody who wants our help. And if they don't want our help, we don't hold it against them. They can go anywhere they want to go. We're just happy to help who's here.
>
> Today, we probably have ten thousand families in our files—and that I think is a conservative estimate. But we may never see a third

of them again because this is a very transient town. People come and go. We're constantly saying, "So long. Hope you come back so we can treat your animals again." And we're also saying, "Well, welcome to the Reno area."

For the two of us, there is no ego involvement anymore. We share everything with each other, the patients and the work, the worries and the fun—and there's no competition.

A wego, by its very nature, must be free of the self-importance of a single competitive individual, and focused on the interdependence of the relationship between equal partners. It must blend those behaviors that once were deemed to reside exclusively in one or the other of the sexes. The development and possession of a strong wego provides the best route to fulfillment in both our personal and working lives. To share possession of a wego is to feel totally human and whole in both your workplace and your personal lives.

Although a wego is the offspring of two egos, it belongs to the realm of values, while egos remain in the realm of drives. As recently as two decades ago, drives reigned over the world of commerce, while values were at a very low ebb.

Professor Jules Henry, armed with the traditional tools of the anthropological field worker, finished his brilliant book *Culture Against Man* (Random House, Inc., 1963) in the spring of 1962. How the world has changed from the time when Henry wrote, "Ours is a driven culture"—a culture in which workers were motivated by achievement, competition, profit, mobility, and the search for security and a higher standard of living.

In 1962, Henry chronicled a world characterized by expansiveness, by the culturally generated drives of competitiveness and achievement, which we pursued with the same fervor as our biological drives of hunger, thirst, and sex. In those days, Henry viewed drives as belonging to the world of occupations. Values, on the other hand, belonged solely to the world of the family and intimacy. As he wrote in *Culture Against Man*,

It is no problem at all to locate jobs requiring an orientation toward achievement, competition, profit, and mobility, or even toward a higher standard of living. But it is difficult to find one requiring outstanding capacity for love, kindness, quietness, contentment, fun, frankness, and simplicity. If you are propelled by drives, the culture offers innumerable opportunities for you; but if you are moved mostly by values, you really have to search, and if you do find a job in which you can live by values, the pay and prestige are usually low.

We have moved a long way from the time when Henry wrote that although values—ideas about good human relations— provide direction, they lacked the compelling power that drives possessed because there was no institutional support for them. Today the recognition is dawning that technology has been pushed to its limits and that if productivity is to be increased it will have to come about as a result of a new concern for people and relationships. Values have come into their own.

Less than a year after Jules Henry wrote *Culture Against Man*, Betty Friedan published *The Feminine Mystique* (W. W. Norton & Company, 1963), setting in motion the women's movement, the most powerful source for social change in our time. In the first stage of the feminist movement, equality for women in the world of business was a major issue.

Those of us who lived through those years of heat between men and women, and between women and women, recall with pain the polarization and estrangement between the sexes. Some men seeking their own liberation from their role stereotypes asked, "Do I really want to continue to climb the corporate ladder? Is there room at the top? And what will it take to be pushed back down?" The ulcers, the heart attacks, the strokes, the mergers, the forced retirements, and the layoffs—it was all beginning to seem as though it might not be worth it after all.

As women entered the business arena and began to climb those corporate ladders, only to crash into glass ceilings, they too began asking those same hard questions as their disillusionment grew. Had they chased the illusion of liberation merely to be imprisoned by assuming those roles their opposite sex had already found imprisoning?

In 1981, Betty Friedan asked in *The Second Stage* (Summit Books, 1981), how it is possible for both men and women to transcend the polarization that has occurred between the sexes and to achieve a new human wholeness, coming to new terms with the family, with love, and with work and transforming the very nature of power itself? The copreneurial movement is one response to the most recent questions and challenges posed by the chief articulator of the women's movement.

From the copreneurs we've met we have learned that there are ways to integrate drives and values holistically into our lives. No longer do drives and values need to exist in the separate realms of the world of work and the world of family and intimacy. These same couples have transcended the polarity that existed between men and women prior to the women's movement because of inequalities between them and because of the polarization that resulted between the sexes from the heat generated by the women's movement. These pioneers are showing us the way to integrate the family, love, and work, and in the process are redefining the parameters of power and sharing it equally between them.

We have said that love and romance, while very real emotions, are difficult to quantify; but when encountered they are easily recognized, and the existence of those emotions is so apparent that they are beyond dispute. The patience and understanding that Tom Dose exhibited for Sharon's need to practice veterinary medicine on an equal footing with him, in a profession that still holds many biases against women, saw him through her nine-month odyssey to seek a practice for the two of them. And Sharon's perseverance during that difficult time came from her realization that their relationship, rather than their two careers, was of paramount importance. "If there wasn't the relationship," she stressed, "there wouldn't even be a need for the career because basically we're working together for the relationship and the same goals."

Tom and Sharon's veterinary practice and personal life clearly integrate all the values that Jules Henry saw as being so separated from our careers and work less than three decades ago— love, kindness, quietness, contentment, fun, and simplicity. As Tom expresses it,

> There really isn't anything that has to do with a business or an outside activity that holds more importance than the marriage or just being happy together. I think we have a lot of romance just in

the fact that our relationship is a very stable one without a lot of frills. And because we know it's stable, all the superficial shows of affection are unnecessary—they really have no meaning to us.

In the long term we show our love to one another by being there day after day and never turning away. We're there for each other when we're needed. All the pats on the butt and pecks on the cheek aren't going to help a bit if the person you're with turns their back on you one day and just leaves you hanging. I don't see how more romantic you can get than spending twenty-four hours a day together with the person you've chosen to be with.

The Doses' life together is characterized by a healthy balance of drives and values—the drives necessary to make their business a success in a competitive profession and the values so essential to the health of any relationship. But the Doses are far from unique. We encountered example after example of copreneurs who, like the Doses, have integrated drives and values into both their personal and working lives— drives that have allowed them to be competitive and successful in their enterprises, and values that can be seen in their respect and love for one another and in the warmth and understanding that so many of these couples exhibit toward their employees. Copreneurs have the capability to invest their work with fun and enjoyment, making the successes of their enterprises all the sweeter.

LETTING GO OF OLD ROLES
AND EXPECTATIONS

It is indeed a significant event to find yourself working in an equal relationship with a partner with whom you also live. The multiple veneers of culturally conditioned male and female roles will quite naturally have an impact on your new working relationship for a time. And no matter how liberated you believe your relationship to be, you will discover yourself unconsciously hanging on to old baggage—roles and responsibilities so pervasively defined in our culture as male or female. After all, you have been conditioned throughout your life to accept them without question and you will quite naturally continue to perpetuate them, transporting some of those roles into your new working interaction and relationship with your partner.

This process of carrying the old into the new will continue until the realization strikes you that many of those old roles and expectations simply do not fit or function in your new copreneurial relationship. With this often unconscious acknowledgment, you and your partner will begin to move toward a more androgynous style, one in which those traits normally associated with either male or female become blended, accepting and sharing roles and responsibilities together. For some this will happen quickly, for others more time will be required. And the roles you assume, both personally and professionally, will not necessarily remain static.

For Sy and Irene of Irene Cohen Personnel Services this process occurred, as it does with many couples, over a period of years. After being married for thirty-four years, Irene observes how she and Sy gradually adopted traits and strengths normally associated with the opposite sex from one another and then applied them to situations in their business. Irene observes,

> I have typically female traits of empathy, motherhood, and mothering. And Sy has very typical male traits—those rigid, detailed, and management-oriented kinds of things. But after being together for so many years, I've learned from him, and he's learned from me. Sy and I have learned to bend. Sy will bend to be a little more humanistic and I will bend to be a little more hard-nosed, and you need to be a little hard-nosed in business.

THE EGALITARIAN NATURE OF COPRENEURIAL RELATIONSHIPS

It was with surprise and delight that we discovered many copreneurial businesses to be enterprises in which there are no clear-cut divisions of leadership based merely on gender. For the most part, the couples we interviewed use individual capabilities and skills as their primary criteria for role assumption, rather than adopting stereotypic roles associated with masculinity or femininity. These egalitarian copreneurs have nothing in common with those couples who conform to an older vision where males hold the reins, controlling all aspects of their businesses, while females are relegated to supportive roles, as exemplified in the old Mom and Pop model.

We frequently observed enterprises in which both partners appeared to be equally powerful. And yet in many of these businesses the female partner had begun without any previous entrepreneurial activity—in some cases without management experience, or even knowledge specific to the new endeavor. Some of these women had been housewives or employed in unchallenging positions that offered little hope for personal growth or career advancement. A similar lack of knowledge or experience specific to their new enterprises did not deter the male half of some partnerships, either.

Traditionally, women have not been allowed to assume active control when men are on the scene. Although capable of assuming full responsibility for virtually any situation, when men are present women have been expected to relinquish control and responsibility. Time and time again, throughout history, women have been held in reserve and used only as a resource, with men assuming the helm. This traditional model was not what we encountered among the entrepreneurial couples we met.

In couple after couple, we found strong women who have emerged as savvy and influential forces within their organizations and industries. Without copreneurial opportunity, there is no doubt that many of these women would not have reached out for the successes they have attained; nor would they have been given the chance to prove themselves at executive and management levels in the outside business world.

Behind every great female copreneur we discovered a strong male counterpart. The males in these relationships were not only able to recognize and draw upon the strengths of their partners; they also possessed self-images that could not be threatened either personally or professionally by their partners' successes and growth. These copreneurial males were men who did not take the helm from their partner, but instead shared the navigation and control of their business equally. These were couples who over time had developed strong wegos between them.

FOUR REASONS WHY
COPRENEURS HAVE THE EDGE

Four basic elements essential for success in any business are already in place and functioning in a healthy relationship. This fact gives businesses run by copreneurs the winning edge. When companies headed by entrepreneurial couples are examined, the elements of *freedom from interpersonal competition*, *communication*, *trust*, and *shared objectives* are found to be the cornerstones of their success. For copreneurs, the development of a wego and the freedom from interpersonal competition are based on the very same elements that contribute to the success of their relationship and enterprise, the elements of communication, trust, and shared objectives.

While business consultants and workers alike would like to incorporate these elements into the business world, and top management often verbalizes such a desire, the absence of effective communication, mistrust, lack of shared goals, and internal competition remain the hallmarks of daily life in the American business scene. Copreneurs have the advantage over entrepreneurs who must work alone, over business executives who must work alone, and over virtually all other workers in their own isolated environments.

Communication

Without communication, co-workers cannot share information, collaborate, negotiate, or lay the foundation for the trust so necessary to the functioning of any successful business. And without trust, misunderstanding and misinterpretation will be daily occurrences, leading to dysfunctioning and ultimate failure.

Entrepreneurial couples have the advantage of communicating both at work and when they are away from the office together. In the office, the daily workload, the demands of staff, telephone calls, and unscheduled interruptions are all part of the normal course of business, and all contribute to rendering problem-solving and creative brainstorming difficult, if not impossible, in that setting. Ironically, in an environment equipped with time-saving gadgetry, all of us have become besieged by plans that cannot be executed, appointments that must be rescheduled, and deadlines that are often not met.

While healthy copreneurs know when to turn their businesses off, they do have a decided advantage in being able to trouble-shoot, plan, or brainstorm either spontaneously or during times purposely set aside or structured into their normal routine, outside business hours.

Irene and Sy Cohen recognized that time specifically for planning and communicating about their business had to be structured into their life away from the office. The Cohens have established a home office, and now each Friday and Saturday are set aside for Sy and Irene to work and talk together in that more relaxed setting. The Cohens call this their "thinking time." The absence of computers and other business equipment in their residence is a conscious decision. Sy explains why they have opted not to bring computers into their home.

> Although that may happen, and we've thought about it, we haven't because then it would be total immersion into tasks and we wouldn't be thinking and talking *together*—we'd be working *alone* at the computer.
>
> We want to just sit down and talk. We've got to talk about the business, without interruptions. And there's very little communication possible during the days in the office. At the office, we each have our own areas of responsibility and there are very few times we can realistically schedule in even an hour to discuss what we're going to do. Since we leave the office too late at night to really sit down and sensibly talk and reason through a plan or problem, the only opportunity we can rely on for this kind of communication is the time we have programmed in to be together in our Connecticut home.

An office in their home is the perfect solution, allowing Sy and Irene to schedule the communication so necessary to oversee any business. Other couples also have learned the value of time structured into their routines in which they can catch up on the day's events, and reflect on where they are and where they are going.

Barry Brooks of Cookies From Home is well aware of the edge he and Susan have over other entrepreneurs as a result of their twenty-four-hour accessibility to one another and the luxury of being able to communicate in settings other than their workplace.

> Although we see each other during the day, we really don't communicate until the evening. It was like that before we worked together, too. We shared everything about our lives in terms of the goings-on of the day, or the work conflicts, or the good news and bad news, and we still do it now.
>
> We share an office and during the day I'll overhear a great phone call Susan might have, or she might overhear something going on with me. But it's at night, I think, that it really happens. It's in the evenings that we get together and say, "Now let's talk about this situation we have." That's when we really communicate and get our work together done.

Trust and Teamwork

Without communication, trust cannot be established and teamwork becomes impossible. In this atmosphere the procedure of covering one's own backside takes precedence over more positive activities. In order to survive in an environment where advancement is no longer an assured reward for work well done, workers in corporate America have become "me" oriented. Their commitment is purely personal—not to a team effort or to a company, but only to their individual careers. This is the logical outgrowth of a business environment where managers have been schooled to place bottom-line commitments above all else—above the company, the product, the consumer, the worker, and ultimately themselves.

In the coentrepreneurial relationship, there is no need to work for personal advancement. With a strong foundation of communication and trust, copreneurs can set aside their personal ambitions and focus together on common goals with the complete faith and knowledge that their partner is working alongside them toward exactly the same objectives.

During most of our interviews, couples reiterated Bruce

Handloff's deep feelings of trust and admiration for Masami, his wife and business partner in their chiropractic practice,

I have tremendous respect for Masami. I feel absolutely secure and trust her one hundred percent. Because we are working for the common good, we keep that in sight above all else. Whatever opinion one may have, the other is taken into consideration. There is no selfishness or competition in the relationship at all.

Shared Objectives

Bruce's recognition of the importance of shared goals within a business was articulated by all of the successful entrepreneurial couples with whom we talked. Each realized that a business is cast adrift unless it has clearly stated goals and shared objectives.

At all levels, from the president on down, an organization must have a common purpose to elicit teamwork and a commitment to accomplishing its goals. When shared objectives are absent or poorly articulated, individuals will place their own goals at the forefront, pursuing their own agendas.

In our own agency, our primary objective is to help each of our clients receive recognition in a competitive business world. We accomplish this through our commitment to excellence and by the passion we invest in our work. We believe that good advertising and marketing is educational, informative, and enriched communication. Through the demands that we place on ourselves, and through our diligent adherence to quality, our goal to create not just good but truly great copy, design, and finished collaterals is transmitted throughout our organization and to each of our vendors and clients as well.

We have found that enterprises headed by entrepreneurial couples have clearly articulated and visible goals that are shared not only by both partners, but throughout the entire organization. The passion that these copreneurs articulate and invest into their enterprises can be seen in the enthusiasm and energy that they bring to their businesses. This passion, enthusiasm, and energy are often so contagious that they are adopted by and become the property of all involved—employees, vendors, and customers alike.

Shared goals can be seen as one of the most powerful engines of success. When copreneurs embark on their projects, they do so wholeheartedly. Their enthusiasm, energy, and faith in their endeavor ignite those with whom they work, assuring success.

Freedom From Interpersonal Competition

Shared objectives, teamwork, and communication can thrive only when interpersonal competition is absent. The organization that structures a competitive atmosphere among its managers and employees creates an environment where individual is pitted against individual, excluding the possibility of any of the three preceding essential elements for business success—*open communication*, *mutual trust*, and *shared objectives*.

Over and over again, copreneurs expressed an unselfish pride in their partners' growth and achievements. Concerning his wife's recent recognition as one of the nation's top twenty female chefs, restaurateur George Germon's fully developed wego allows him to proudly express his feelings regarding the honor bestowed upon Johanne. "It was perfect timing. We couldn't have asked for a better situation. And I certainly rode the tail wind that Johanne created for the two of us. I just appreciate any recognition we get for our restaurants." Like so many of George's copreneurial counterparts, his comment reflects the supportive and noncompetitive attitude characteristic of a fully developed wego.

While business consultants and authors are urging companies to adopt open communication, trust, shared goals, and freedom from interpersonal competition, couples in successful relationships quite naturally put these building blocks to work. By the very nature of their personal relationships, copreneurs begin their business partnerships with a head start, having the elements of success already actively operating for them. It is quite logical for them to pass these working styles on down through the business organization as their enterprises grow and prosper.

CHAPTER

8

The Business of Your Business

Money, or the lack of it, is the primary psychological stumbling block that keeps most people from ever going into business for themselves. This is unfortunate, because we believe that anyone with determination, faith in their enterprise, and belief in their own abilities can launch a successful venture. In fact, beginning a business with too much money can be more unhealthy for a new business than starting out "lean and mean."

Beginning your business lean can be to your advantage. Without the false sense of security that easy capital often engenders, you are forced to go to work smarter, faster, and without the luxury of false starts. Nothing will get your product or service into the marketplace more quickly than the need for cash flow when readily available money is in short supply. Running lean and mean is the acid test of any business. When you are forced to operate with a low overhead, scrutinizing every purchase and keeping your eye on the balance sheet at all times, you will develop a keen sense of control and business acumen that can't be learned in any school.

YOU DON'T NEED MONEY TO MAKE MONEY—
YOU NEED DETERMINATION

Almost any business can be started with one hundred percent leverage if you know how to handle the debt load. If you begin your business with a healthy wad of cash from your own savings, *you* are loaning money to *your* business with the expectation that you will recover that loan and, in the process, earn a healthy profit. Thus you are starting your venture with a debt that you owe to yourself. If you don't have savings to draw upon, or a home to mortgage, and must turn to outside resources, you are *still* beginning your business with a debt—the only difference is *who* is to be repaid. While debt, particularly owed to someone else, can keep you awake at night, and the financial juggling act will keep you on your toes during the day, that is a normal and expected part of beginning your own venture.

Business failure resulting from undercapitalization is a myth. What is a reality is business failure resulting from poor planning, mismanagement, or the lack of commitment to give sixteen or eighteen hours a day if that's what it takes. Money in itself is never a substitute for creativity, clever strategy, or just doing what needs to be done when it needs to be done.

When money is in short supply, "sweat equity" can always make up the deficit. Many more successful businesses are founded with this kind of equity than with a healthy bankroll. The business world is filled with the success stories of entrepreneurs who started in their garage or basement and went on to turn their enterprises into multimillion-dollar success stories. These entrepreneurs were not lucky, although opportunity most certainly plays a role in success. Every single story has one thing in common—the founder's belief in what they are doing and the drive to make the business a success. Thomas Jefferson once remarked, "I'm a great believer in luck. The harder I work the more I have of it." But to be able to take advantage of "luck" you have to be smart enough to recognize it and put it to work for you.

Remember that with only $200, a family recipe, and a burning determination, Liz and Nick Thomas began their gourmet mustard company, Chalif Inc. Nick had made a career selling insurance and believed that selling their mustard would have to be easier. After Liz talked him into making their first batch of Chalif mustard, the couple made their initial sales call in December of 1981 to their local cheese shop. Nick remembers walking in and explaining to the buyer why they were there. "Oh my God, not another mustard!" the woman declared. "Can't you see I'm busy? Don't bother me. Come back some time after the first of the year. It's ten days before Christmas and you couldn't have picked a worse time." But Nick was undaunted as he started to twist the lid off a jar of their mustard, saying, "Well, we'd be happy to come back, but would you at least be willing to taste it and tell us whether we have a viable product? We really don't know whether we've got anything here. We know we like it and our friends like it, and we'd like your professional opinion."

Reluctantly the buyer dipped her finger into the jar of mustard, put it to her tongue, and immediately called someone from her staff over for a second opinion. After they had both tasted it, they looked at each other and the buyer said, "I'll take two cases." That just happened to be the Thomases' entire inventory, which was sitting on the back seat of their car. Not only did that first shop buy all the mustard they had made; it paid for it on the spot and in cash. The Thomases immediately bought more ingredients—and Chalif Inc. was in business!

Following their local success, the Thomases resolved to get their product on the shelves of Zabar's, New York's famous West Side food store. Accomplishing that goal took all of the bulldog tenacity that Nick had developed at New York Life Insurance Company. After months of persistence—phone calls, letters, and repeated sales calls—Murray Klein, President of Zabar's finally relented and agreed to an in-store tasting demonstration, stating, "You have until two o'clock and if it doesn't sell, that's it for Zabar's."

The couple arrived from Philadelphia in a driving rain with thirty cases of mustard in their car. Liz was crestfallen, fearing that the rain would keep customers away from the store. However, what she didn't know was that when it rains in Manhattan, even more customers pack into Zabar's normally crowded store. In five hours the Thomases sold every case they had brought with them. And at two o'clock the floor manager advised them that Chalif mustard was going on the shelves.

For Liz and Nick, it wasn't money that brought about their success—it was the belief that their mustard was unique and their commitment to doing whatever needed to be done to get their product on the shelves. Even today, the Thomases continue their venture with the same drive that made the impossible a reality, bringing about a complete change in their fortunes. Their now-famous mustards and condiments can be found on the shelves of gourmet markets across the country.

Claude and Donna Jeanloz founded The Renovator's Supply, their enormously successful direct-mail and manufacturing enterprise, with the proceeds from the sale of a home they had renovated in Quebec. Ted and Joyce Rice used their life savings —money that had been earmarked for their retirement—to build that first mobile bakery, which ultimately mushroomed into a fifty-million-dollar franchise operation.

Sy and Irene Cohen launched Irene Cohen Personnel Services with a modest $5000 in the middle of a recession, even though everyone told Irene, "This is a crazy time to start a business." And Sam and Libby Edelman made the decision to part with some personal property which had been purchased with investment in mind, including their beautiful Dutch warmblood horse, to obtain the seed money for their fashion shoe firm, Sam & Libby, California—an enterprise that after nine months in operation had back orders totaling three and a half million dollars.

When Bruce and Masami Handloff decided to open their own chiropractic clinic, as a newly married couple without equity in a home or any savings they had to be particularly resourceful. Bruce discovered the Hebrew Free Loan Association, which provides interest-free two-year educational and business loans to members of the Jewish community. The only catch was that the couple had to obtain six Jewish cosigners and submit a business plan in which profitability was forecast within the first year. After some scrambling, Bruce came up with the six cosigners—his Uncle Mel, his Aunt Corinne, his childhood synagogue choir teacher, and the remaining three followed in quick succession.

With that interest-free $5000 loan, Bruce and Masami were able to obtain a second loan from their local credit union for $20,000. The same month they opened their doors for business, Masami gave birth to their first child by emergency Caesarean; the bill was a whopping $10,000! The couple had no health insurance and a negative cash flow of $138 that month. However, their business was in the black—not in one year as they had projected, but by the end of their third month of operation. The only way that Bruce and Masami could open their practice was to borrow all the money they needed—a one hundred percent leverage of their enterprise.

FROM TERMINATION TO DETERMINATION

We established our advertising agency within twenty-four hours of our simultaneous termination. The very day we were fired, as we were clearing out our desks, we began an animated discussion of how we were going to make the dream of running our own advertising agency a reality. And on the way home we dropped by our favorite gourmet market to buy the best bottle of Chardonnay on the rack. When our three children returned home from school that afternoon they were surprised to discover the car parked in the driveway and their parents sitting on the floor in the middle of the living room, with their glasses of wine, excitedly discussing future plans and making notes on how to accomplish them.

Anthony, our oldest son, recalls that as they walked up the path to the house and saw the car, our daughter Kimberly became apprehensive. All three children knew of the difficulties we had been experiencing at the office, and they realized the possible implications of their parents being home so early in the afternoon. "Oh, God, they've lost their jobs," Kimberly said to her brothers. However, Anthony and Elliott, Frank's sons by his previous marriage, didn't share her anxiety. Both of them had watched their father, on more than one past occasion, establish and run other successful businesses. Since Sharan had not been entrepreneurial before our marriage, Kimberly, unlike the boys, had no such experience from which to draw reassurance.

Coming through the front door, Kimberly was filled with dread, and while her brothers headed nonchalantly to the refrigerator for milk and sandwiches, she asked, "What are you doing home?" We told the three of them that we had indeed been fired, but in the next breath quickly filled them in on our plans to strike out on our own. Kimberly remained skeptical. "Do you really want to work together in your own business?" she asked her mother in a worried voice. And Sharan's response was a very positive "Yes, we really do!" That night the five of us celebrated the beginning of our enterprise at our favorite Chinese restaurant and topped the evening off at the cinema.

Our first hurdle was to locate the necessary capital to tide us over during the critical start-up phase of our agency. With little equity or savings, we would need the funds to support our family of five—money for housing, utilities, food, transportation, and other necessities. In addition to our personal needs, our new venture would require office equipment, stationery, and supplies, as well as a self-promotional brochure. Traditionally, service businesses can often be launched on a shoestring. However, we believed that a brochure that conveyed the philosophy and panache we wanted our agency to possess was the best business investment we could make—despite advice from colleagues who cautioned against spending a considerable amount of limited capital on that item.

We knew that it would be at least six months before we would see any black on our balance sheets. The day after our termination, Frank called his mother in Los Angeles. With Frank on one line and Sharan on the other, we filled her in on the previous day's events and our plans for the future. She could hear the excitement in our voices and recognized that the time was right for us to strike out on our own. She also recognized that we were without sufficient equity or capital to launch a new enterprise, and without hesitation—or our even asking—she volunteered, "Well, we'll just have to find the money, won't we? Let me know what you need and I'll see if I can help."

Within a week we had developed our business plan and a careful budget that would see us through our first six months. In less than two months, Frank's mother had refinanced her house, and loaned us the money for our venture. Barnett/Associates was under way. Now we must stress that our benefactor is not a woman of any great means. However, her generosity and faith in our abilities allowed us to make our dream a reality, and we recognized the risk she was assuming to her own security and the financial obligation we were undertaking as well.

We were fortunate to have sufficient space in our home to set up comfortable offices at one end of our large living room. Knowing that we would eventually be moving into permanent offices, for continuing identity we established a post office box and remote business telephone lines that were call-forwarded to our home from the phone company's central switching office. With a permanent post office box and business lines that could eventually be moved to another location, we were able to proceed with the design of our elaborate brochure with the assurance that it would not be outdated by an incorrect address or telephone number when that move was made.

As an advertising agency, we were keenly aware that our image was of paramount importance. We began at once designing our own logo and corporate identity. And when it came to the design of our self-promotional brochure, we pulled out all the stops, using techniques that were new to our industry—electronic imaging and a silk-screen process that allowed us to spot-register a plastic coating over selected areas, creating a striking illusion of depth and dimensionality.

As we worked with our vendors, the printer, silk-screener, paper supplier, typesetter, and color separator, our enthusiasm became contagious; and as their excitement for our collaboration grew they became "enrolled" in the project. As a result, some vendors provided their services at their cost, just to have their name in the credits, and samples to show their customers. Before we had even made a sales call, we were building a reputation in our industry as an agency worth watching, while at the same time establishing our credit lines and relationships with vendors.

In the end, our creative collaboration between technologies and people resulted in a brochure that won an international design award and is still the principal collateral in our agency, one that has helped us land many of our most important accounts. Without the participation and contributions of our vendors, we could never have afforded to produce that piece. Our award-winning brochure cost $9000; but if our suppliers had not joined us in the production, it would have come in at well over three times that price. The enrollment that character- ized our vendors' enthusiasm for that first project has been carried forth into all our subsequent creations, enabling us to set a level of excellence that has become the hallmark of our organization.

While we did have a business plan when we began our venture, it was a document that quickly became outdated. The rapid growth of our agency came as a pleasant surprise. Like so many other copreneurs we began our business during an eco- nomic slump. In fact, one of our motivating forces was the realization that Silicon Valley firms were cutting back their in-house advertising departments, while *ADWEEK* was simulta- neously reporting that these same companies were letting their agencies go. Yet we knew that the high-tech companies still needed to promote their products and would have to turn increasingly to small, creative, and competitive agencies, deal- ing with them on an à la carte basis. And that's exactly how we built our firm, chipping away at the big guys project by project.

From the outset, we carved for ourselves a highly specialized market niche in the high-tech arena. The success of our organi- zation can be attributed directly to our agency's ability to translate our clients' technical products into an easily under- stood communication to the customer. This has always required a delicate balance between the boredom that bits and bytes can elicit and the other extreme of gagging our audience with glitz. Because of our ability to communicate clearly and technically for this industry, we soon found our agency fully booked and happily immersed in projects ranging from the production of technical seminars to user manuals, annual reports, technical data sheets, articles, catalogs, promotions, product development, and packaging.

MAKE THE OPERATING SYSTEMS
YOUR FIRST PRIORITY

Within the first two weeks of prospecting, we found ourselves landing accounts and becoming fully engaged in projects that were more complex and on a grander scale than we could ever have anticipated at the outset. The importance of business plans and projections is undeniable. However, setting your systems in place, almost from day one, is equally imperative.

Regardless of the product or service your company will provide, before you design or sell your first widget, bake your first pizza, or consult with your first client, you must plan the systems that will allow you to deal with vendors, purchase and control inventory, price your product or service, write your first order, bill your first sale, deliver your first widget, and deposit your money safely in the bank. Your first priority must be setting up your business so that when you do take that first order, everything else will fall into place behind it. If you don't have your ducks in a row from the very beginning, you'll find yourself trapped in a game of "catch-up" that may never end, and which most certainly will stretch you and your endeavor to the breaking point.

During our first three months in business, all of the systems for an efficiently run advertising agency were set in place—accounting, record-keeping, and estimating procedures were established, and an outside bookkeeper, who is still with us, was hired on a monthly retainer. Before we made our first sales call, our organization was fully operational. We had established our banking relationship, lined up outside vendors, set up the accounting and billing procedures and cycles, designed and printed our internal forms, implemented a computer-based system for estimating project costs, designed our company logo, and produced our business cards and stationery as well as our self-promotional brochure. We had made our *own* business our *first* account.

The two of us felt like race horses straining at the bit, ready to join the race and jump into business. But we reined ourselves in, resisting the temptation and the sense of urgency that told us we should be out on the street hustling. Instead, for those first ninety days we focused all our energies on laying the groundwork and establishing a solid organizational foundation upon which our firm could operate smoothly and grow.

DON'T POSTPONE PUTTING
APPROPRIATE TECHNOLOGY TO WORK

Just as we advocate beginning your venture together as partners from the outset, so do we strongly advise that you utilize those technologies appropriate for your business at your first opportunity. We located our agency on Monterey Bay, a forty-five-minute drive over the rugged Santa Cruz Mountains from Silicon Valley. Knowing that a great deal of our time would initially be spent making sales calls and presentations away from the office and telephone, we hired an answering service and purchased a message beeper.

Knowing just how crucial the telephone is to any business, when we had selected the answering service we felt was right for our agency we visited their office and introduced ourselves and our business to all the operators on the staff. We wanted to be more that just a number and a voice to them; and we wanted them to be more than just voices to us.

It is our firm conviction that small businesses should avoid answering machines like the plague. And when those same businesses grow into large organizations they should resist the temptation to install elaborate automated electronic systems that connect callers to one tape recorded voice after another. Nothing is more frustrating to a caller or deadly to a business than a phone system that distances potential and existing customers from real human contact. As customers, we avoid doing business with firms that require us to leave recorded messages without ever speaking to a real human who can respond at the moment of the phone call. No matter how efficient these businesses *believe* their systems are, any system that costs you customers is neither efficient nor smart!

While we're at it, we also become quite peevish when forced to listen to music or commercial radio stations when we are placed on hold. If you are on hold for any length of time, hearing a few songs or several commercials only reminds you of just how long you've already been kept waiting. Musical taste is so individual that no one style will be enjoyed by everyone. It's much nicer to have silence and the conscientious individual who returns at appropriate intervals to inquire if they might be of some assistance to you, or to ask if you still wish to hold or would like to leave a message.

Our beeper paid off a thousand times over in its first week of use. We had done a small direct-mail promotion in Silicon Valley, and one of the first beeps we received was from a company responding to our mailing. We returned their phone call from the next freeway off-ramp, scheduling an appointment for the next day. As a result of that meeting we landed our first project for a high-tech firm—a client that was to become our largest account.

While the beeper allowed us to respond quickly, we soon tired of trying to speak or hear over traffic and low-flying aircraft in roadside telephone booths, or from smoke-filled hotel phone banks sandwiched between sales reps yelling into their receivers. We agonized over the cost of purchasing and using a cellular car phone. What a waste of time that was! From the first day the phone was installed, our car became a highly efficient mobile office. We quickly realized that a car phone is not a luxury but a necessary tool for our agency and, we suspect, for many other businesses as well.

Today's technologies enable even the smallest businesses to compete with the giants. We deliberated over the purchase of every piece of equipment, weighing the pros and the cons, only to discover that once the equipment was in use, we could not imagine how we had operated without it. We have learned that if a particular technology is necessary, our only consideration is

how to finance bringing that technology into our organization.
Once we learned that lesson from our cellular car phone,
decisions to purchase such items as computers, a high-speed
copier, fax machine, laser printer, desk-top publishing systems,
and computer software were made comfortably and easily.

A DILEMMA JUST WAITING
FOR A TECHNOLOGICAL SOLUTION

For Brian and Mary Harvey of Rakestraw Books in Danville,
California, just the right computer hardware and software allowed Mary to return to a business she and Brian had founded
fifteen years earlier. The couple, who have known each other
for nearly four decades, have been married since 1970 and are
the deans of our copreneurs—Brian is seventy and Mary is ten
years younger.

Before becoming a bookstore owner, Brian had been the
director of advertising and public relations for a manufacturing
firm in Southern California. When the company relocated to
Manhattan, Brian bailed out to look for a new career. He and
Mary relocated to Northern California, where for a time, they
worked together at a private school, Brian as assistant to the
director and Mary as a secretary—a position she did not enjoy.
Mary eventually left the school to work for a dentist, and two
years later, Brian was fired.

Before Brian's termination, Mary had clipped a small classified ad with the titillating caption, "Build a Better Bookstore."
Six months later, when Brian was unemployed with no prospects for the future, Mary brought out the clipping and said,
"Let's go see about this bookstore system." As she recalls,

> Clipping out an ad like that is totally uncharacteristic for me. I
> never do this. We drove to Ross, California, where the developer of
> a unique shelving and inventory system lived, and was advertising
> his product in the *Wall Street Journal*. We were the very first people
> to buy that system.
>
> As a couple, we are very spontaneous and we never look back.
> We've worked very well that way together because neither of us
> worries about decisions. We make them and live with them and this

is characteristic of the way both of us operate. We purchased the system and rented our first store in one day. We didn't do any market research. We simply said, "Let's open a bookstore." We just took all the money that we had, every cent we could pull together plus what we could borrow, and did it.

In January we made our decision to own a bookstore, and by the end of March we were open for business. We had agreed that it would probably take as long as two years for the bookstore to produce enough revenue to cover the rent for our retail space and the mortgage for our home.

However, in less than two years, there was enough cash flow for us to get by.

Mary and Brian worked together in the bookstore six days a week for ten years. During that time they gained a reputation in the retail book trade among their customers, book representatives, and publishers as one of the finest stores in the San Francisco Bay Area. They also expanded twice, moving from their original store with only 900 square feet to their third location with a spacious 2100 square feet.

Early on, Mary had made the decision to computerize the bookkeeping and purchased a personal computer to maintain the records. However, all of the inventory, ordering of books, and aging of their stock were done by hand on index cards. Record-keeping in a bookstore can be a nightmare, and more than one owner has been buried alive by the mountains of paperwork that all bookstores generate. To keep ahead, Mary was arriving at work by seven o'clock each morning to control their inventory. In addition, the Harveys had to hire clerks to assist in keeping the work up to date and their clientele happy.

Four years ago, feeling that they weren't making enough money to survive, Mary left the business to sell real estate. Although she was a successful real estate agent, she never truly left Rakestraw Books. She still maintained the bookkeeping and would drop by every day, ordering books and directing the staff as to how she would like her bookstore run. It was a difficult time for the couple.

It was a strain with my not liking the way the bookstore was being run because Brian would feel defensive when I was critical. I would tell the staff what to do when I saw things being run in a way I didn't like and that caused problems too. Nobody likes to be told what to do by someone who is only there an hour or so. That's just not the way you run a business.

When Mary told Brian that she was going to attend the Northern California Booksellers Association meeting in October of 1987, Brian remembers saying as she went out the door, "Don't buy anything," and Mary's reply was, "Okay, I won't."

> When she came back, it slowly became apparent that Mary had committed to the Ibid computerized inventory system for bookstores. When I asked, "How much?" she said, "Twenty thousand bucks." And my reaction was, "We're going to have to sell a whole hell of a lot of books to get that back."

However, Mary's decision to computerize the bookstore solved their dilemma and allowed the couple to work together again profitably as soon as it was installed. The system allows the two of them to run their business with only part-time help during evenings and weekends and additional staff during peak seasons. Even Brian, who balked at learning to operate the system, is now an avid convert.

> At first it got tense and sticky and I hated everything. Initially I hated every god-damned minute of it because learning to run the computer all but made childbirth seem a pleasure—and believe me, we're well beyond the child-bearing years. But gradually I came around and all our part-time people came around as well.
> We're both happy to be working together again; whatever money Mary made in real estate really wasn't worth it. When Mary finally took all of her real estate signs back to the agent, I felt the promise of a great sense of relief. And more and more as each week goes by, I'm even more pleased that she's not in the real estate business any more. She was very good at it and she enjoyed it, but it seems to me that she likes our bookstore much better.

GIVING STRUCTURE TO YOUR ENTERPRISE

Couples today have grown accustomed to taking huge financial leaps in their stride—purchasing automobiles, financing the costs of higher education, and mortgaging homes that now cost more than the average family could have hoped to earn in decades not so very long ago. And in community property states, where goods, property, and the assets of a business acquired during a marriage belong equally to a husband and wife, the name of one or the other spouse on a contract or title may seem of little importance. However, when you have determined to become a copreneur, the form your business takes will play an extremely important role in how you can grow and expand your enterprise.

Basically, the structure of your business will come from one of three straightforward choices: sole proprietorship, partnership, or corporation. The business form you choose for your enterprise will depend upon your unique circumstances, the advice you obtain from your tax and legal consultants, and the structure with which you and your partner feel the most comfortable.

Sole Proprietorship—Unlimited Liability

Operationally, when we established our advertising agency we began as equal partners. In actuality, however, our business was a *sole proprietorship.* Today it has grown into a California corporation with a third full and equal partner and is legally known as Barnett/Chu Associates doing business as Barnett/ Associates. We began as a sole proprietorship because of the ease that form of business offers initially. To begin our business, we needed only to obtain the necessary tax identification numbers and file a fictitious name statement with the county. Because we established our business in an unincorporated area, we were not required to obtain a local business license.

Sole proprietorships are by far the most popular form of business in the United States and Canada. They are the easiest to start and the easiest to dissolve. All profits are received by the owner, and all liabilities as well. Income taxes are filed on personal returns, and there is no financial division between the individual and the business.

The largest drawbacks to being a sole proprietor are the total liability you must assume and the limited access to capital for growth. When a sole proprietor borrows money, it must be as a personal loan, and individual assets, automobiles, equipment, and real property are at stake. And if a sole proprietor is sued, all personal possessions are at risk.

Partnership—Equal Liability

A *partnership* involves two or more individuals who pool their money, abilities, and skills in a business, dividing profits or losses according to a formula based on a predetermined agreement. This form of business is far more complex than the sole proprietorship. While the sole proprietor is liable for all debts his or her business may incur, each partner in a partnership is personally liable for all debts of their enterprise. Thus, in a partnership, you could find yourself responsible for expenses that were beyond your control or even your knowledge.

While many small enterprises begin as sole proprietorships without any legal counsel, you would be ill-advised to enter into a partnership without legal advice or written agreements. Still, this business form appeals to many people because it is viewed as being easier to enter into than forming a corporation. However, legal fees can often run as high as those required to establish a corporation.

Corporation—Limited Liability

Two-thirds of the copreneurial enterprises we encountered are structured as *corporations*, and there is a good reason for this. Because a corporation is separate from its owners, the liability of the shareholders is limited only to their participation. A corporation is its own entity—it can borrow money, contract for services, and be bought, divided, or sold. By its very structure, a corporation represents the collective interests of the shareholders, directors, and officers, not the interests of any one individual.

As a legally recognized entity, a corporation has, in the words of one jurist, "neither a soul to damn nor a body to kick." It is without question the most convenient business form to accommodate growth, minimize conflict, and incorporate change within an organization. While a corporation is run by people, it does not depend upon the functioning of any single individual.

Since the Tax Reform Act of 1986, it may be more advantageous for some businesses to establish a Subchapter S corporation. This flexible form of incorporation provides limited liability under the corporate umbrella, while affording certain tax advantages that in the past were available only to businesses operating as sole proprietors or partnerships. Subchapter S corporations should be seriously considered for small and medium-sized enterprises, particularly during the start-up phase if initial losses are anticipated.

Since there are several forms of corporations, including *for profit*, *nonprofit*, *professional*, and *close corporations*, it is important for you to consult both your attorney and your accountant to determine which form will be most advantageous for your particular business. If you elect to form a corporation, remember that it must be established as a *real* business, not merely a front set up to reap tax benefits or minimize liability. Your enterprise must be a viable operation, transacting business under its corporate umbrella. If it is not, you may well find the state or federal government "piercing the corporate veil"—filing action in court and stripping your business and its participants of the limited liability that legitimate corporations enjoy.

In any corporate structure you must have Articles of Incorporation, the guidelines under which you will operate. You will issue stock to shareholders, elect a board of directors, appoint officers of the corporation, and hold regularly scheduled meetings with recorded minutes of those proceedings.

The impetus for transforming our business from a sole proprietorship to a corporation came about when we decided to bring a partner into the firm. The limited liability the corporate structure offered, the flexibility for growth, the mechanism for diversification, and an organizational matrix within which the interests of all parties could be equally represented provided an ideal form for our new triumvirate.

DETERMINING YOUR SHARE OF THE PIE

We have always chosen to be equal partners, sharing owner-ship, responsibilities, and tasks on a fifty-fifty basis. When we brought our partner into the agency, we maintained the equality of ownership, dividing the shares of the corporation into thirds.

For a variety of reasons, many copreneurs elect to share ownership on a basis other than an equal split. The percentage of ownership, however, does not necessarily have anything to do with the compensation the two partners take from their ven-ture. For many complex reasons, usually focused around tax and retirement considerations, copreneurs do not always choose to draw equal salaries. Often accountants will advise copre-neurs to pay one partner a substantially larger salary than the other in order to reduce the second partner's Social Security withholding.

Regardless of how the copreneurs we met divided the owner-ship of their enterprises or apportioned their salaries, there was never any question concerning the equality between the partners and their individual commitments to their businesses. Most of the businesses we encountered were owned equally by their founders. We found only two enterprises that were divided along a fifty-one/forty-nine percent split. And in both these instances the unequal division of ownership seemed to strike an emotional chord in at least one of the partners of each enterprise.

Leslie Kadis, MD, and his wife, Ruth McClendon, LCSW, are psychotherapists with practices in San Francisco and Aptos, California. In addition to their individual private practices, Les and Ruth work together as coconsultants in The Institute For Family Business, which they established with a third partner to meet the needs of individuals and families involved in family enterprises.

As experts in their specialty, the couple also travel throughout the world conducting workshops to train other professionals in their methods of family therapy. Les, who was an anesthesiolo-gist before becoming a psychiatrist, still maintains a practice in that field, working one day a week in the operating room. Despite their busy schedules, the couple coedit the international section of the *American Journal of Family Therapy,* and co-authored *Chocolate Pudding and Other Approaches to Intensive Multiple-Family Therapy* (Science and Behavior Books, Inc., 1983).

When they began working together, Les joined Ruth in her clinical practice, which involved the training of psychotherapists throughout the world. Les was in private psychiatric practice when Ruth, who was leaving California for four months to teach and train psychotherapy professionals in Europe, called her psychiatric consultant to find the best family therapist in the area to take over her patients. The consultant recommended Les, who agreed to absorb Ruth's patients into his practice.

Upon Ruth's return she needed a cotherapist for several major workshops, and invited Les to join her. That was twelve years ago, and ever since they have been combining their individual specialized skills into a unique complementary and supportive style of cotherapy. When Les joined Ruth's practice it was basically her business, operating under her own corporation. Ruth remembers that once Les joined her enterprise,

> Together we gradually changed the form of it so it became ours. We eliminated some of the things that we had done, and added new things, and certainly changed the theoretical orientation because Les was primarily a systems-oriented person and I was more a Transactional Analysis-Gestalt person. We combined those orientations, coming up with our own model of doing therapy. From there we gradually moved into building The Institute For Family Business and consulting with family enterprises.

As a medical practitioner, Les had continued to maintain his medical corporation. However, on the advice of their accountant, Ruth gave up her corporation and the couple placed their business under Les' corporation. The Institute For Family Business, however, remained a partnership. Les observed that there were sound accounting reasons for operating under his medical corporation.

> I'm seven years older than Ruth and so retirement will kick in earlier for me. In addition, it was just much more favorable to put all the assets into my corporation rather than hers. However, the

only way it could remain a medical corporation was for me to retain fifty-one percent of the shares.

It was a soul-searching experience to come to that decision and for Ruth to end her personal involvement in her own corporation. I really respected her because I know it was a hard decision. For me, it didn't make any difference, but it certainly did for Ruth. At the time she said, "That's because you're a doctor and a man—of course it doesn't make any difference." And she was probably right about that, but I felt really clear that if she wanted to continue our business within her own corporation, it really didn't matter to me.

Today, Ruth acknowledges that even though they operate as equal partners in all respects, the fifty-one/forty-nine percent split does have emotional implications for her.

Actually, if I had it all to do over, I would never do it again—not in any way, shape, or form would I give up my identity and become subsumed under Les' corporation. From a practical standpoint it's been smart, it was an economic decision that we both agreed to—but economics are very different from emotions!

With Sy and Irene Cohen of Irene Cohen Personnel Services, their fifty-one/forty-nine percent partnership came about as a result of very different circumstances. And in their case it is the female partner who holds the controlling shares in the organization. As Irene told how *her* business became *their* business, it was clear that Sy is not at all bothered by his minority position.

Sy joined the firm, at first as an equal partner. But today, he holds forty-nine percent of the company and I have the remaining fifty-one. The reason for that is very interesting. At the time we negotiated our partnership I was reading in the women's magazines— you've got to remember that in the early seventies women's liberation was at the forefront in the news—and these stories were all about women whose husbands were leaving them with nothing.

And I read all this and said to Sy, "Let's renegotiate. I really want fifty-one percent. I started the company and my name is on the door. I want the security that fifty-one percent will bring." Sy really had no problem with that and readily agreed.

In spite of their forty-nine/fifty-one percent agreements, Sy and Irene, as well as Les and Ruth, are obviously equal decision-making partners in their ventures. Partnerships, like marriages, to succeed must maintain a fair balance in which one individual does not exert absolute control—regardless of how the business is divided. And for many enterprises there may be advantages to being a minority-owned business with the female partner holding the controlling shares.

However you decide to divide the pie and whichever form of business—sole proprietorship, partnership, or corporation—best fits your needs today and the anticipated needs of your enterprise tomorrow, as you begin fitting the pieces of your organization together, give careful thought and consideration to how those same bits of the puzzle might also be dismantled. Part of your planning should be the anticipation of the unexpected as well as of growth and success. Your plans should also include provisions for bringing in partners, selling the business, or simply closing the doors.

Our lives are marked by change; and no matter how committed we are to our enterprise in its present form, the future will bring new opportunities. Growth can only come through change, and the single most characteristic feature of the entrepreneurial spirit is its capacity for nurturing those fluids in which change can flow. Change is the lubricant for growth.

Remember that you don't have to be a financial genius to launch your venture and succeed in the business world. Don't be intimidated by the fact that you don't know everything there is to know about finance and running your business. You are more than capable of learning everything you need to know to have a firm understanding of all the really important aspects of business—and you can always find someone to do what you really can't or just don't want to do yourself. Keep in mind that the *real* experts, those with the MBAs, can usually be found sitting behind a desk in someone else's company, not out starting their own business.

In fact, take your lack of expertise as a good omen—it just might result in an original, innovative way of accomplishing your goal. The expert advice is there for the asking—your

accountant or your attorney will be glad to help for a fee—but
don't overlook the business section of your neighborhood bookstore or library. You will find that many of the answers you need
are right there on the shelves, authored by people with practical
experience.

9

Letting Others into
Your Relationship

As our agency grew, we recognized that our individual
capabilities were finite. And, with the management of
staff added to our already over-burdened workload, each
new employee seemed to create more, rather than less, work for
us. Our days were reserved for dealing with clients and administrative tasks, which left only the evenings for the creative
process so necessary in the world of advertising. We would
break for dinner, spend some time with our children, take a
deep breath, and begin working again. Each day was really two
full working days.

From the beginning of our enterprise we routinely worked six
or seven days a week, each of us devoting eighty to ninety hours
a week to our venture. By the end of the second year we were
exhausted and, looking back over the past twenty-four months,
realized that we had worked the equivalent of more than four
years during that period. Time for our creative collaborations
was being sacrificed on the altar of administration.

Increasing the size of our staff had not been the answer, and
our problem seemed without resolution. Since cloning ourselves

was impossible, the only reasonable solution was to bring into our firm someone else who could function at our level. The problem with that, however, was that we couldn't afford to pay the salary such a professional would command. But, as so often happens, an opportunity presented itself when it was least expected and most needed.

For two years we had been nurturing a relationship with Donna Loevenich, a product marketing manager for one of our largest and most valued clients. The easy rapport that had been established almost from our first meeting had evolved into a relationship of mutual admiration, trust, and friendship. Privately, we had often observed that if there were anyone we would like to bring into our organization, it would be Donna. However, we knew that was impossible for at least two reasons —we would never jeopardize an account by pirating away a valued employee, and we knew that Donna's current salary was beyond our present means. For those reasons we never seriously contemplated approaching her, and she had no idea of our wishful thinking.

One day we were working on a project with Donna in her company's cafeteria when her boss approached the table. His pained expression alerted the three of us that he had been engaged in serious battle. He asked to speak privately with Donna and we were left alone, conjecturing on what could possibly be so dire. We couldn't imagine what was going on, and the more we tried to guess what was happening, the more uncertain we felt.

When Donna returned to our table, her eyes were filled with tears as she announced that she would not be able to continue our meeting because she had just been laid off. Before she could collect her materials both of us were saying, "Wait, you can't leave yet, we've got to talk to you. Do you know what you're going to do? Do you have any plans?" But Donna was in a state of shock, and she needed time to compose herself and collect her thoughts.

We continued that meeting with Donna's boss, bringing him up to date on the project, but our thoughts were elsewhere. The layoff had been massive, and as we walked through the mazes of cubicles throughout the huge facility we witnessed dozens of employees packing their belongings into cartons and still more in tight huddles, discussing their plights and exchanging hugs and handshakes. It was a depressing scene, but not an unfamiliar one in Silicon Valley. The employees who were left behind were expressing feelings of guilt and insecurity, and those who were leaving were simply devastated.

As we were driving back to our office, we called Donna at home on our car phone. When she answered, the composure she had managed to regain was evident in her voice. We told her how much we had always admired her abilities, and asked her to consider joining our firm—perhaps as a partner.

Now it may seem strange that we were so willing to give up the sole control of our agency, but we had learned from experience the importance of working together on a totally equal basis, and the concept of control was not as important to us as being able to bring in the right person as an equal. Frank had owned his own businesses from the time he was a teenager, and we had both reached the point in our lives when ownership wasn't the issue. What mattered most was doing what we loved doing, and doing it in a fashion that wouldn't result in burnout. Bringing Donna into the firm, we felt, would make that possible.

We were well aware that the salary we could afford to offer Donna would not be commensurate with her past employment history and abilities, but we hoped that offering her a partnership might provide sufficient incentive for her to take our proposal seriously. As we talked to her, while negotiating the freeway rush-hour traffic, we discovered that from the very beginning she had been impressed by our operation, and expressed interest in exploring ways in which we could work together.

Within two weeks we began our new working relationship, cautiously at first, bringing Donna into our operation initially as a consultant. From the first day she began working for our organization, it was clear that she could make a tremendous contribution, bringing to our firm the extensive experience she had gained from working in the corporate arena for a decade, in addition to having owned her own computer consulting firm in Germany. What a relief it was to have an equal working with us, one who required no hand-holding or monitoring, and who approached her work with a savvy bottom-line awareness.

At the end of the first month, the three of us agreed to hire a mediation attorney to facilitate discussions that might lead to a partnership agreement. We considered the possibility of hiring two attorneys to represent our separate interests, but opted instead for mediation rather than an adversary approach to exploring our future relationship. Each of us had the trust to place our collective future in the competent hands of a single legal professional who represented the interests of all of us equally—Donna, Sharan, Frank, and the business itself.

Those sessions were characterized by an openness and candor between us that remains to this day. The agenda for those exploratory meetings included a frank discussion of our personal goals and professional objectives, as well as an exhaustive list of topics covering virtually every aspect of our business and the industry we were serving.

Out of those creative and thought-provoking exchanges was forged a partnership agreement based on open communication, trust, freedom from competition, and clearly articulated and mutually shared objectives, with consensus as the agreed-upon mode of decision making. Donna was brought into our firm as a full and equal investing partner, and it was determined that incorporation best served our individual needs as well as the future needs of our growing company.

During the course of those meetings Donna also discussed her plans with her family, close friends, and colleagues. Not surprisingly, many cautioned her against placing herself in the position of a minority partner. More than once she heard, "It'll be two against one," or "Two's company and three's a crowd."

Cultural biases against couples working together as employees are very real. The workplace has not been an environment in which a positive view of working couples exists, and unfortunately models of working relationships are derived from that arena. Management traditionally assumes that couples, because of their unique emotional, financial, and legal interests, will work toward serving their own ends rather than the overall good of the company. And in today's corporate world, where many hold an attitude that they are working to further their own individual interests rather than those of the organization, the concept of real teamwork, based on equality, is totally foreign.

Coming from a corporate background, it was not surprising that Donna's colleagues would hold a partnership with an entrepreneurial couple suspect, believing them to be an impenetrable power base. But fortunately for the three of us, Donna didn't see it that way. In fact, during our entire working relationship she had never viewed the two of us as a single unit, but rather as two professional individuals. We formed our corporation using Donna's maiden name, Chu, in its title. We became Barnett/Chu Associates, doing business as Barnett/Associates for continuing identity.

Donna's joining our firm brought about an important psychological shift in our own view toward Barnett/Associates. The faith she had placed in the future of our company, as well as the respect she expressed for the two of us as *individual* professionals, made us feel "real"—dispelling once and for all any feelings we might have been harboring that we were, after all, just a Mom and Pop agency.

Bringing our future partner in on a consulting basis had allowed Donna to test the waters and to lay the groundwork for our relationship before making a commitment to invest in the company. Coming from a corporate environment, she relished the informality of a small organization. And we soon realized that the structure of a large corporation, which Donna was bringing to our operation, was a real asset. In addition to her skills as a project and marketing manager, we quickly discovered that she had equally impressive administrative skills, which promised to free us for more creative tasks.

We were fortunate to realize that our strengths did not lie in either business management or administration. Many entrepreneurs become estranged from their own enterprises once they begin to operate in areas where they possess neither the skills, the talent, nor the inclination necessary for success in a business grown beyond the founder's abilities. We recognized our strengths, as well as our limitations and, thanks to our capable partner, we have been able to continue to build our business around them, doing what we do best and enjoy most.

Today, the two of us are responsible for the creative direction of our agency, including the writing of all copy; the development of the central themes for our clients' marketing promotions, as well as the creation of concepts for direct mail and media campaigns, sales and promotion incentives; and all art direction. Donna has assumed total responsibility for general administration and financial operations, including purchasing, and accounts payable and receivable, in addition to acting as our agency's research analyst. The three of us share some responsibilities, often acting in concert as account managers—estimating project budgets, scheduling campaigns, reviewing the status of accounts, working with the staff and outside creative people, and attending press checks together. By bringing Donna in as a full and investing partner we didn't *lose* control—we *gained* control of our agency, our time, and our future.

From our own experience, and from the experience of couples we have met, we have learned that partnerships work well for some copreneurs, while others, like Harvey Clar of Harvey Clar Auction Gallery, state that they would never consider sharing their business with anyone else.

> Partners, I think, are a tough situation. I might consider a partner in real estate, but that's an investment type partner, not a partner who's involved in running the business on a day-to-day basis. I've heard of very few partnerships that work for a long time. There always seems to be an outside problem between the partners' families or wives that leads to a breakup. Even in situations where it *should* work—where one guy's in the manufacturing end and the other is financial—and there shouldn't be any jealousies, the wives can ask, "Why is *he* doing this? Why is *he* able to go to the shows? *They're* always in New York. You're stuck in the office and *I* don't get to go anywhere." I would never let anyone into our gallery as a daily partner. I really think that would be very hard.

Copreneurial relationships, by their very nature, can be closed and impenetrable to employees and prospective partners —but it doesn't necessarily have to be that way. Copreneurs *can* extend the openness that exists between them, allowing it to filter down throughout their organization.

EXTENDING THE BOUNDARIES
OF MUTUAL DEPENDENCY

While the majority of the copreneurs we interviewed are going it alone, twenty percent have found the advantages of bringing partners into their firms sufficient to be willing to share ownership and control of their enterprise. These couples have extended the mutual dependency that exists between them beyond the boundaries of their own relationship.

When Nick and Liz Thomas came to the early realization that their business would eventually become more than just a cottage industry, and since they were not in a position to afford any personal liability, they quickly incorporated their company. Within weeks of their incorporation and initial sales a close friend, who had received his usual holiday gift of mustard, with its handsome new Chalif label, called them on the day after Christmas.

> Liz and Nick, you know I've always loved your mustard, and I think your new label is terrific. Marketing the mustard is a great idea. But I know you don't have the capital, and you know I do. There's nothing that would please me more than to write you a check for one hundred thousand dollars, or whatever it takes to launch your business. But for heaven's sake, let's do it right.

The couple's immediate response was to turn down his offer, saying, "Oh no, Joe, we're not going to give up a part of our company. Thanks, but no thanks." However, their friend was insistent. "Well, at least meet with me to discuss doing a business plan. I know Nick has experience in the management end of business, but he doesn't know anything about a start-up company. Let me help you."

With that, they began four months of weekly meetings with their friend, who later became their partner. In the meantime, reorders were coming in and Liz and Nick were scrambling to keep up with them. After dinner they would clean up the kitchen, starting each night around seven, making mustard until the early hours of the morning. Nick had no time to find new accounts, and all of their revenues were immediately reinvested into the ingredients to keep their mustard in the stores. It didn't take long for the Thomases to see that they would have to move their business out of their kitchen to increase production and to resume family life on a normal schedule. Liz recalls when the realization sank in that setting up a manufacturing facility, no matter how small, would take capital.

We had to have someplace that we could call an office and a factory and we had to have salaries. At that time my mother was still paying the mortgage on our house and every penny we made was going back into the business. So we finally took Joe up on his offer. I think his initial investment in Chalif was one hundred and twenty thousand dollars, and for that we gave him thirty percent of the company. And at that time everyone was saying "That's crazy, he should have gotten seventy percent and you should have gotten thirty." But he is a good friend who we've known since the early sixties, and Nick is the godfather of his oldest son.

Sure, we would have liked to have kept the whole thing for ourselves, but that just wasn't realistic. Maybe if we were in our twenties and starting this company our objective would have been to start the Chalif dynasty. But I think at our age we've got our priorities in a lot better order than that. And we'd rather have ten percent of a big pie than one hundred percent of nothing. I don't think either of us has ever been as interested in tremendous wealth as in the quality of our life.

You have to have money to do things in business. We needed a filling machine, we needed a facility, and we needed to draw a salary. So it became obvious that we had to have a front man. Naturally, you don't want to give away the store, but we were lucky in finding someone who understood our situation and was wealthy enough on his own not to say, "I have an ego here to satisfy, and not only that, but the Penn Business School says I walk in here and get ninety percent."

Joe Hill, the Thomases' partner, today sits on the board of directors of the corporation, but allows Nick and Liz a completely free reign in the operation of their successful business.

And when Chalif Inc. has needed additional infusions of capital, Joe has always been there. Since Joe is a vice president of a local brokerage house, he isn't a working partner. However, the Thomases keep him abreast of everything that goes on. Nick understands what it is that makes their partnership work.

> There has to be complete trust between partners. They have to know you and you have to know them—it's just like a marriage. I think we're lucky. We've had an open, direct line of communication and Joe has always had complete knowledge of what we are doing. He's very good at asking a great deal of questions, but has never said to us, "You do this" and "You do that."

All the elements were in place to make this partnership work for the Thomases—friendship, explicit trust, and free-flowing open communication. And most important, neither Nick, Liz, nor Joe had an ego that got in the way of the partnership or that required taking absolute control.

Without their partner, getting Chalif Inc. off the ground might have been more than the Thomases could have managed. With him, their gourmet mustard quickly went on to gain national recognition and distribution, and in 1983 was voted the best domestic gourmet product of the year by the National Association for the Specialty Food Trade.

Ted and Joyce Rice opened their first permanent T.J. Cinnamons Bakery in January of 1985 in the Ward Parkway Shopping Center in Kansas City, Missouri. From that location, the story of T.J. Cinnamons took an incredible turn and began to make franchising history. In July of 1985 Kenneth D. Hill, a nationally recognized food and restaurant expert, became a partner with the Rices, forming Signature Foods, Inc., as the parent company for the T.J. Cinnamons Bakery concept. Ken was named president and chief executive officer, and began at once to develop the company's national franchise program. Ted became chairman of the board, and Joyce was named vice president.

By September the franchising program, which was to catapult T.J. Cinnamons to a fifty-million-dollar operation, had begun; and within the first seven months of the formation of the partnership the enterprise had grown from its original bakery with only six employees to a network of twenty-three bakeries employing over a thousand nationwide. Today, there are over two hundred T.J. Cinnamons bakeries across the country. Without their partner's franchising expertise and the professional franchise support staff that he brought on board, the Rices acknowledge that their venture would undoubtedly have taken a dramatically different course.

The decision for copreneurs to bring in another partner must depend upon their goals and their willingness to share their personal creation with someone who is outside the bounds of their close relationship. In the case of Ted and Joyce, their intuition, belief in their product, and faith in their partner's abilities transformed their enterprise from a small Mom and Pop bakery to one of the nation's leading franchise opportunities.

When Johanne Killeen and George Germon opened their first restaurant, Al Forno, in Providence, Rhode Island, they did so without a partner. However, there was a time when the nationally renowned chefs thought that Al Forno might not take them where they wanted to go professionally. During that period they began searching for a second location. Johanne remembers how they kept bumping into Josh Miller and Tom Bates.

> Josh and Tom's expertise was in the liquor business, and we had known each other for a long time. They were also looking for a location for a night club. George had worked for Tom many years ago in his contracting business, and the first restaurant we had worked in together was one that Tom had built. The four of us decided to combine our efforts and that's how The Hot Club and Lucky's started. However, George and I still retained the outright ownership of Al Forno.

The Hot Club, a bar with a very simple menu, was run primarily by Josh and Tom because of their expertise in liquor, while George and Johanne assumed most of the responsibilities at Lucky's. However, Josh later began to manage Lucky's dining room, freeing the couple to concentrate on the kitchen and to relax about what's going on out front. In addition, Josh has assumed responsibility in the office for setting up the computer, and has taken on some of the office duties. And Tom has taken over the accounting for both the bar and the restaurant. George describes the relationship among the four partners as unique.

At some point one of us will want our own way on one particular thing and when that occurs, we've all agreed that the other three just say, "Okay, that's the way we'll do it." We feel that if something is *that* important to one of us, then the other three *should* back them all the way, no matter what.

I think it's important to have a third or even a fourth person you can count on who will free you to have a life and to grow. Otherwise, you can become consumed by the business. We've learned to delegate and our partners are willing to do anything—it doesn't matter what it is. If we need someone to work in the kitchen we know they'd be there and they'd do it. Sure, they'd be scared, but they would do their damnedest to get through whatever crisis we were having. There's a teamwork that we have among the four of us and we rely very heavily upon it.

With Tom and Josh we can leave both of our restaurants for a week to travel, and that's where our growth is—having a partnership allows us to be away and feel comfortable rather than anxious.

When the partnership was being formed, Tom and Josh assumed that because George and Johanne were married the business would be split into thirds. However, George was adamant that the division be equal among the four partners. Today, George says with pride,

Johanne is the power behind the group. She has a great deal of input into the organization and things happen because of her. Josh and Tom now realize that she's a performer and a person who's able to accomplish what she sets out to do and we all benefit from it. It's a great partnership and we're very, very lucky.

Like George and Johanne, we also realize that having an equal and capable partner frees us to schedule time away from the business, knowing that it is in experienced and competent hands. During our extensive cross-country interviews for this book, there wasn't a moment when we doubted Donna's ability to handle any situation or project back at the office. In fact, without her, we doubt that we would have embarked on a project as complex and time-consuming as *Working Together.* Having a partner has allowed us to expand our horizons and to grow personally at a speed that would not have been possible without her.

Each of the copreneurs introduced here had different motives for extending the boundaries of their mutual dependency to include partners in their enterprise. In our own case, we were motivated by the realization that we were simply stretched to our personal limits and that adding staff did not relieve our workload. We needed someone to join our firm who possessed many of the same skills and commitment to excellence, as well as talents and knowledge that would extend beyond our experience and areas of interest. After Donna joined our firm, we discovered that our agency's capabilities had been increased and that the limits of our individual creative boundaries were extended.

Although Donna joined our firm and made a financial investment in the corporation, her infusion of capital did not play a major role in our motivation for adding a partner. For Liz and Nick Thomas, however, bringing a partner on board with the financial resources to back their start-up venture was critical in getting their project off the ground. And while their partner plays a crucial role in an advisory capacity, Joe Hill's strong wego allows him to trust the day-to-day operations of Chalif Inc. to the Thomases.

In the case of Ted and Joyce Rice, the expertise and franchising experience of their partner, Kenneth Hill, moved T.J. Cinnamons in an exciting and expansive new direction. The Rices' keen vision and faith in the viability of their product, coupled with their partner's superb mastery of the food and restaurant industry, resulted in T.J. Cinnamons rapidly becoming the nation's largest specialty bakery chain.

George Germon and Johanne Killeen's partnership with Tom and Josh has allowed the couple to expand from their original trattoria, Al Forno, to their now equally famous second restaurant, Lucky's, as well as The Hot Club. But, and perhaps of even greater importance, their partnership has provided the personal freedom for George and Johanne to grow professionally and to expand their already extraordinary culinary repertoire. When we met with the couple in April of 1988 Johanne had received recognition earlier in the year as one of the nation's top twenty female chefs. Only two months later, the restaurateurs were again recognized, this time as *both* being among the top ten new chefs in America.

EXTENDING AN OPEN AND SUPPORTIVE MANAGEMENT STYLE TO EMPLOYEES

As we have seen, some copreneurs have successfully extended their open and supportive style of working together to include partners outside their close and intimate relationship. Many of the couples we met, both with and without partners, have demonstrated that it is possible to manage their employees in a style that employs the same valuable tools—freedom from interpersonal competition, communication, trust, and shared objectives—that have allowed their copreneurial relationships to succeed. When it comes to employee management, there is a clear choice—an entrepreneurial couple can remain a closed power base, or they can choose to extend their open and supportive style of interacting to include their employees.

Since a remarkable number—nearly two-thirds—of the copreneurs we met began their enterprises right in their homes, many brought employees into that setting as well. The eventual size of the enterprise seemed to have no relation to home-based start-ups. Many large and successful operations literally began on their founders' kitchen tables. And some copreneurs have opted to keep their businesses in their homes, while others quickly outgrew that setting.

When employees are brought into a home-based business, it is quite natural for an informal atmosphere to prevail. Often the founders' children are present, and there is little in the home that is considered off-limits to employees—usually only the bedrooms. If the business remains in the home, the informality will continue. And, as is most often the case, if an enterprise moves into a more traditional business setting, the camaraderie and sense of togetherness between the owners and the original staff will carry on as the business grows. As long as those original staff members remain with the company, that early kinship remains a part of the work setting, and through them it can flow down to newer employees as they join the firm.

It hasn't been that many months since Sam and Libby Edelman moved their fashion shoe firm out of their home and into offices in San Carlos, California. Sitting in the backyard of their house, we discussed what it had been like to blend business and family under one roof. For Libby, having two preschool children and the business together had been a strain.

> We took over one room of the house and that was where we all worked. But I felt it was hard on the kids because they weren't allowed in where we were working. It drove them crazy and me crazy. We also started just having too many people here and too many cars in the driveway. I had to leave this place, and we moved the business out after four months.

For Sam, however, it was a real luxury to work out of his home, sharing the personal atmosphere with Libby and the rest of the staff. "I would have stayed here for one whole year. It didn't bother me at all. I loved being here. And I thought having lunch here was just the greatest thing. That was a difference between husband and wife."

Even though the Edelmans have moved Sam & Libby, California into offices away from their home, their house remains a focal point for many business activities. The couple make sure that when their design associates from Italy are in town, as well as the company salesmen, they stay at the house rather than at an impersonal hotel. And new employees who are moving into the area become welcome house guests.

Because many of Sam and Libby's staff had worked with the couple before the formation of their venture, close relationships had already been formed. Building on those relationships, and on the intimacy that resulted from working even more closely together for four months in the couple's home, has bonded the staff to the founders and their business. As Sam explains,

Our company is a modern company in many, many ways. We want to develop an entrepreneurial spirit at every level of the company. Because most of the people who work with us had been with us for a number of years at Esprit, everybody feels like Sam & Libby is *their business*. We've never asked anybody to work late hours, but we have one woman who works six days a week—it's like the business is her baby too. She wants it to be successful and she knows that by putting her all into it all of us will benefit. And I really think that's the spirit of the whole company.

And our staff knows they will be rewarded. Around here if it's time for you to get a raise or a bonus, *there ain't going to be any committees*—there's not a lot of red tape. If we have to save the money somewhere else, like long-distance phone calls, that's okay. But if you're part of our entrepreneurial team, you'll be rewarded.

At Sam & Libby, all the staff is totally involved with everything that is going on. Recently, when the start-up firm went through a tough period, Sam was able to keep everyone focused on the positive aspects of their growing enterprise. As Libby tells it,

One Friday when we'd had the worst week—everything that could go wrong, did go wrong, it seemed—Sam said, "Let's have a meeting." At that meeting he said to all of us, "Let's not forget we just had three great things happen—the shoes fit, the boxes worked, and the ships didn't go down on their way up from Brazil. You can't always think of the negatives. We're out of the house, our phone system is great, and the copier works. Whatever it is that is positive —that's what it's all about." I think we share a lot with all of our employees—we're all on the same team.

The closeness of the Edelmans and their staff was driven home by Sam's observation that if something happened to their new venture,

Not only would Libby and I want to continue working together, but our core team would stay with us as well. We're a real team and we would sell ourselves to another company or just start over again. We have a formula and we're going to make it work. The idea of splitting up would never occur to me.

While most copreneurs who begin their enterprises in their homes eventually move them to more traditional business settings, Ian and Betsy Weinschel of River Bank, Inc. have made a conscious decision to keep their video production studio in their farmhouse. From that tranquil setting, an hour from Washington, D.C., during election years, Ian and Betsy become the political tacticians in their candidates' commercial wars that are played out on our television sets at home in time slots measured in just seconds.

Working every other year in the political arena, the Weinschels and their film crew share an equality that can be attributed to many years of working closely together. "Our relationship with all the film crew is really very good," Betsy explains, "because we basically grew up in the business together. Even now, it's the same film crew that we have worked with for twenty years." And because their editing studio is located in their large home, the couple's four children have close contact with the employees. During political campaigns their staff expands to eight or ten employees, and as Betsy acknowledges,

> The main problem is when an employee leaves for one reason or another, the children will say, "You know, I really liked them. Why did we have to get rid of them?" It's harder for the children. They feel like the staff has been brought in as part of the family and suddenly, when they are no longer working here, the children are asking, "Did you get mad at them?" Then finally, you'll understand that what they must be saying is, "Are you going to get mad at me? Am I going too?"

Although the Weinschels are a very close couple, they have extended the boundaries of their relationship to encompass their staff, allowing them into the inner circle of their immediate family. Ian and Betsy have found a balance between work and family that successfully integrates those two worlds.

Close relationships between copreneurs and their staffs are obviously not predicated on beginning a business in the home, although working in that more intimate setting can certainly contribute to an openness between owners and employees. Donna and Harvey Clar did not start their enterprise in their home, but clearly have developed and mastered the management skills that have resulted in a low staff turnover and a caring interaction with their employees. In fact, one of their employees has been with the Clars for twenty-one years, having worked with them before the establishment of Harvey Clar Auction Gallery. Others who have been with the Clars since the beginning of the gallery exhibit a loyalty that is not often seen in business today. Harvey gives his crew considerable leeway, and believes that,

> When you let people plan their job and do their job, and they know that you have given them the autonomy to perform on their own, they won't let you down. I expect a lot from them, but I'm not on their backs all the time. I know they'll get the job done. I think you get in trouble with employees when you feel that you've got to be after them all the time, that they can't handle the job, and you've got to tell them to do every little thing. I'll certainly tell them if I don't think they're doing something right, or if I want something done in a certain order, but it's their job and I know they can do it better than anybody else.

The warmth that exists between the Clars and their office staff and crew results from the kindness and consideration the couple extend to each other and to each employee. Donna and Harvey never disagree between themselves in front of their staff. When disagreements do arise, they retreat to their office and discuss it, "sitting down, with the door closed." And if a staff member needs a reprimand, it is always given privately, never in front of another employee. Harvey told us that it is not uncommon for them to become involved in the private lives of their employees by extending help whenever needed.

> I work well on a two-way street, where it's give and take. I get along with that very, very well and I don't deal well with people who just take and never give. I find that very hard. Our crew knows that if they have any problem whatsoever, Donna and I will help them solve it. If they have a medical problem, although we have medical coverage for the staff, or if anything happens with their kids or if they just need a few hundred bucks for an emergency—whatever is needed—they're never going to get turned down at home base.
>   They know they've got support from us no matter what happens. For instance, Manuel brought his wife in to talk to Donna about

how they should go about buying a new house. And she told them all the things they should do and all the steps they should take. She told them what they should look for, where they should apply for financing, and she even made some telephone calls for them.

We do that for the employees and they give back to us in other ways. I know that if I called the guys right now and said, "I need you at three o'clock in the morning—I've got a deal and I've got to get it picked up," there is no doubt in my mind that they would be there and make sure the job got done. Everybody on our crew is really giving, and we give right back.

Copreneuring provides a unique opportunity to develop a management style characterized by the nurturance and support of employees and close interactions between owners and staff. While this same opportunity certainly exists for entrepreneurs working alone and for other managers in corporate and business settings, because copreneuring is based on teamwork between two individuals who have developed mechanisms for working together, there already exists an internal model for supportive interaction that can be extended to include other partners as well as employees.

The basis of copreneuring is teamwork; because of the success of the copreneurial relationship, many coentrepreneurs do not hire employees—they hire team members. Also, many copreneurs have structured their enterprise to suit their own ideal of a business they would like to patronize, just as they manage their employees in the manner in which they would like to be supervised if their roles were reversed.

WHEN YOU LET SOMEONE IN
AND PHASE YOURSELF OUT

When Boyd and Felice Willat of Harper House, Inc. began their company, their vision was to create their product in an environment in which everyone could work to their highest potential. The couple even hired a stress management consultant to give nutritional advice and massages to their employees. In those early years, Boyd notes,

We were experimenting with new social environments that could produce a product and counteract the impersonal world of business. That was actually a part of our operating style as a company. In looking back on our management style we now realize we placed too much emphasis on the personal environment rather than on the efficiency of the company.

We were trying to run one big extended family. We really worked at it. We used to have honesty seminars and had consultants on staff who would encourage communication on that level. And we were always trying to *repair* people when they started to grow out of their jobs, rather than replace them with truly trained professionals. There is a certain mechanics to running a business and it has to do with skill—you really have to have people who are trained to do the job they're hired for. We didn't understand that then, but we certainly do now.

Felice and Boyd founded Harper House, Inc. in 1980, in their rambling family compound consisting of a main house, two smaller cottages, and a garage. Located on Harper Avenue in West Hollywood, California, the complex had been built in the 1920s by Boyd's father, Irvin Willat, a silent film director for his star and bride, Billie Dove.

Felice and Boyd both came from the motion picture and television industry, where Boyd had been a successful art director and set designer for such films as *Raise the Titanic* and *Ordinary People* and Felice had been a production coordinator on a number of television shows, including "Welcome Back Kotter" and "The Julie Andrews Show."

The original inspiration for Harper House came from a journal-writing workshop Felice had taken with Ira Progoff, a key figure in the journal-writing movement of the 1970s. After completing that course Felice developed her own journal to create a feedback calendar so she could chart rhythms and unusual events in her daily activities.

Friends who saw her journal were impressed—they hadn't seen anything like it before. And Boyd marveled at its simple genius. Encouraged by such positive response from family and friends, Felice asked Boyd, who had also worked in advertising, to enhance the journal with his graphic ability.

From their prototype the couple developed a book called *The*

Keeping Track Journalog and sold it to a San Francisco-based publisher, who in 1978 marketed fifteen thousand copies. Believing they had other products that could be equally successful, the Willats developed and submitted *The Keeping Track Sourcebook* which, to their surprise, their publisher rejected. As it turned out, that rejection was a stroke of luck for the couple.

Combining Felice's organizational talents and Boyd's technical and artistic abilities, the Willats formed their own company, designing and manufacturing distinctive, high-quality vinyl folios and binders in vivid, exciting colors. They developed the *Day Runner* organizer, a unique, loose-leaf, refillable, personal planning and information management system, which they brought to market in 1982.

Their product was much more than just a combination address book and calendar—it provided a simple, effective way for individuals to manage the complex details of their daily lives. It was an instant success, effectively creating the organizer product category. Harper House's dramatic growth had begun—an extraordinary feat, considering the conservative and cautious stationery marketplace. The young upstart company was introducing strikingly colored fifty-dollar products into a marketplace accustomed to grays and browns with ticket prices normally under ten dollars.

From an initial investment of just $12,000, Harper House has grown from a small cottage industry to an international multimillion dollar company marketing its products to over six thousand retail outlets in this country and internationally through a network of distributors. The *Day Runner* is now available in five languages, is marketed in eleven different countries around the world, and is used by over two and a half million devoted customers.

More than any other copreneurial enterprise we encountered, the early years of Harper House were centered around its founders' home. The business gobbled up room after room and building after building of the Willat family compound. Before the couple finally relocated Harper House to larger facilities in 1985, only three upstairs bedrooms remained private from the business, and the house was buzzing with family and nearly seventy employees.

The Willats' enterprise had simply overrun the entire two-thirds of an acre on which the compound was located. The main production was in the garage, cartons were shipped from bedrooms, salesmen called clients from the dining room, and the receptionist greeted visitors from her desk near the grand piano in the living room. All the available rooms in the cottages were filled to overflowing, while automobiles clogged the front yard and delivery trucks arrived at all hours of the day and night to drop off materials and to pick up outgoing shipments of *Day Runners*.

Initially, Boyd and Felice employed family members and neighbors. With such a close association between their immediate family and their employees, traditional personnel management became transformed into a more intimate interaction. The couple routinely invested twelve to fourteen hours a day in their enterprise, and Felice recalls that, "In the beginning, the employees took care of the baby, the dogs, and the garden."

When we toured the large manufacturing facility in Culver City, California, that now houses the corporate headquarters of Harper House, we could see that the friendship and respect remain between Boyd and Felice and their employees. However, it was also clear that more traditional management styles have evolved, replacing the intimacy of those early years on Harper Avenue.

Today, Harper House is more successful than ever, but Boyd, who still holds the position of chairman of the board, is no longer managing the company. In a scenario that is not uncommon when an enterprise grows beyond the management experience, capabilities, or desires of its founders, Boyd and Felice made the decision to hire professional management. As Boyd explains,

When we began as entrepreneurs, we were in close contact with our product and people. But a company needs systems and controls, and very seldom do entrepreneurial couples think of building these when they embark on their enterprise. More often, they focus on the needs of the marketplace that can be transformed into a product or service, not on building a business structure. But there is a shift in thinking that takes place as a organization grows that begins to focus on the importance of building in standard operating procedures. And this thinking doesn't occur in the beginning.

Without the insight of having run a big business, I made the classic mistake of a young entrepreneur in a tightly held company. As Harper House grew, we needed skilled people so we hired employees who had the necessary skills we were looking for. But we failed to hire people with management know-how, because *we were the management*. And then we grew so big, so fast, that we required outside capital in order to put the machines and systems in place needed to track marketing data, sales, inventory, and receivables. It is possible to be successful and need money, because money is the faith that lives between suppliers and customers.

In the end, we went through three generations of employees and changed every member of the management team. Finally, I had to *fire* myself. I hired a CEO who was a known commodity with a proven track record in the corporate world. At that time, Harper House needed professional management and credibility more than it needed me.

My job became a piece of change I could trade or sell to take our company to the next level. I had to replace myself as the principal manager. I am still chairman of the board and Felice is still president of Harper House, but I had to give up a certain amount of control and some of my personal vision for our product to buy stabilization and credibility in the money market.

It was almost impossible for me to be a professional manager when I was so close and so emotionally involved with our product. It was very seductive to try to solve all the problems myself. Our CEO, on the other hand, always hires someone else to solve problems and he *must* do that. His job is like the distributor on a motor, sparking all the parts and keeping them in rhythm.

I have watched him take the long-range view of our company. Where my concern had always been immediate and short-term, he realized that the business itself was another product and his primary objective was to build that product called "the company." I had a vision for the product—he had a vision to build the company to a certain profit margin.

The lesson I have learned is to *hire* people to solve problems—not to be *the* problem solver. And today, I could become the professional manager for another company—but not my own.

There is a danger in letting others in—managers or partners with power and autonomy to think and act for themselves—and Boyd Willat acknowledged that he took a "high-rate risk" when he sought and obtained the best management possible. While knowing that his role in Harper House would change, he also realized the value of objective management and company credibility, without which he might lose the creation he and Felice had worked so hard to build.

When the Willats let someone else into their company, they had not anticipated that it was the beginning of Boyd phasing himself out and Felice remaining in her active role as company president, but that is what evolved, and today their company is prospering because of Boyd's courage in bringing in professional management and his willingness to step aside.

KNOWING WHEN TO QUIT

There are situations when more than just stepping aside is called for. A couple should also know when the time is right to let go of their business altogether. It is wise to have a plan for leaving the business behind, almost from the very beginning of a venture. And while it may seem strange to develop a contingency plan for severing the ties to your own business, many enterprises are founded with the goal of eventually being sold to a larger operation.

You should be aware of the circumstances when getting out of your business is the most appropriate thing to do—if the world is knocking at your door with offers to buy you out; or if the big guys become your competition and begin to overpower you with heavy marketing and advertising dollars; or if retirement is drawing near and you need to diversify your investments.

Copreneurs should not feel that their enterprise need live on forever. As long as it is serving the needs for which it was founded, and as long as the founders are enjoying running the business, selling out or just closing the doors should not be a consideration. But if you find yourself in constant conflict with your partner over business matters, or if the thrill of business is gone for the two of you, then it may be time to start investigating alternatives—including ending your participation in the enterprise.

DON'T GET CAUGHT IN A TUG-OF-WAR

Because copreneurs are two individual people, they must be alert to a tendency to "divide and conquer." Children will often pit one parent against the other, testing their resolve, and some employees may attempt to work one owner against the other if the couple are not clearly committed to supporting each other's goals and directives.

Copreneurs can also create confusion by transmitting mixed messages or continually countermanding their partner's requests, orders, or policies. Many couples have overcome this tendency by having their employees answer to only one of the partners. Others have developed the practice of referring an employee who is questioning a direction or order back to the partner with whom it originated. However, when this method is employed the partners have a responsibility to touch base with one another to assure that the employee is not caught in a loop between them and that questions are quickly dealt with and resolved.

In traditional work settings, employers and employees often deal with each other on a single dimension—the world of work. It is the rare employer, in fact, who views the employee as a whole human being—a worker, a parent, a child, a husband or wife, an individual who is made up of multiple roles, many of them overlapping and conflicting and which, from time to time, will most certainly hamper their role as a worker.

There is, after all, something wholesome and natural about a couple working together. Their persona is more complete than that normally presented by management in the world of work. They are owners, they are managers, they are husbands and wives, they are parents, and they are much more. Coming from that perspective, if they hold an accurate self-image, they should understand better than anyone else how roles can conflict, overlap, and sometimes interfere with one another. If they have the insight to acknowledge and understand this about themselves, they can recognize it in others as well and be more human in their dealings with subordinates. Copreneuring offers a unique model for business and management—one which, far from being closed and self-serving, offers unlimited opportunities for expanding upon mutual strengths and dependencies.

PART THREE

Living Together As Copreneurs

For copreneurs, there are no boundaries between work and home or work and pleasure.

10

Business Is Business— You Can't Take It Personally

Perhaps the most common misperception concerning couples working together is expressed by the statement, "How can you work together all the time without fighting? If we were together that much, we'd be at each other's throats day and night!" This perception concerning relationships in general, coupled with the ambivalence Americans have toward anger, constitutes one of the major biases against couples working together. This view is based on the assumption that anger between individuals is unhealthy and destructive, and therefore it would be unhealthy and destructive to work together because the more a couple are together, the more they will fight.

Many Americans embrace anger because they view it as an expression of assertiveness and, at the same time, fear it either within themselves or when they become the focus of another's anger. Americans have a conflict with anger, and far too few of us differentiate between that emotion and aggression, rage, or even hatred, which are all too pervasive in our society. The manifestations of uncontrolled and often violent emotions surround us. We witness them daily on our freeways, read about them in our newspapers, and watch movies in which mindless violence takes the place of meaningful plots. By their sixteenth birthdays, most American children will have viewed eighteen thousand "murders" on television.

To add to the confusion, aggression, which is often mistaken for anger or assertiveness, is believed to get results where other more positive behaviors such as kindness and understanding do not. The "Rambo effect" is an outgrowth of Americans' acceptance that anger or aggression can restore our sense of dignity and justice. Many in our culture learn to assume a stance of *mock anger*—a posture taken to assert ourselves and gain control over situations or other individuals. Given our culture's use and misuse of anger, is it any wonder that people fear anger when it occurs with a loved one?

EXPRESS YOUR ANGER WITH ANGER— AND DO IT HONESTLY

Anger, like love, has an enormous capacity for fostering positive change and growth. Because many in our culture do not understand that there is a difference between anger and the *uncontrolled* expression of deep emotion, they have not learned how to use anger appropriately. However, it *can* be an effective and sometimes necessary tool for communication. Anger can be used for destructive purposes or it can be a building block of communication, which is the foundation of every healthy relationship. It is a *process*, not a disease; it has a cause and a result. And the only way to deal with your own anger is to express it honestly.

The copreneurs we met have made a commitment to a twenty-four-hour closeness in their business and personal relationships. There are no barriers between these individuals—and there is no game playing. Couples who work together can't hide from one another, and they can't place other people, their jobs, or financial problems between them.

Most important, because of the trust and commitment between couples who work together, copreneurs know that when disagreements, problems, or arguments arise their relationship is not in jeopardy. And where both partners are strong individuals, disagreements and anger should be anticipated as an essential part of the process of working together.

As action-driven individuals, copreneurs have learned that the cause of arguments is not of primary importance. They understand that the task between them is not just to arrive at a mutual understanding of why anger has arisen; what is important is to decide on an appropriate course of action in response to the problem, and to follow it through. When anger arises, what you do about it depends upon how you view it and on the context of that emotion in your relationship.

Men and women in the workplace express emotions quite differently. Men will generally suppress their emotions, maintaining a "cool" façade, often allowing only anger to surface. Women, on the other hand, usually feel more comfortable suppressing their outward expression of anger, but allow other emotions free reign—tenderness, nurturance, sadness, elation, and dependency. As a mirror of society, the workplace fosters the subordination and dependency of women upon men, placing men in the role of controlling adults and women as dependent children.

Copreneurs, on the other hand, are engaged in a relationship characterized by mutual dependency, dealing with each other on an adult-to-adult basis of equality. Because of the trust that exists in their personal as well as their work relationships, copreneurs are freer to experiment and to express a fuller range of emotions, the men testing and becoming comfortable with traditionally female responses, and the women trying on and assuming roles of control that have been all too often reserved for men.

For Sharan, anger has taken on a very different meaning over time. Since we have worked together, and because of the absolute equality that exists between us, Sharan is now more comfortable expressing her own anger and dealing with Frank's anger as well. The threat that any fight might escalate to a separation is so far removed from reality that our arguments can now be focused on their cause, and our energies concentrated on resolution. Today, when disagreements occur, we have learned to communicate meaningfully with each other within a safe context of mutual dependency, and to grow from each new interaction.

From our own experience and the experience of other co-preneurs, we have developed the following guidelines for transforming anger into a powerful communication tool. Anger is a transaction, a process, a way of communicating, and it has the power to become a positive rather than a destructive force in our lives.

1. Express anger with anger.

When you experience anger, make sure at the outset that what you are angry about is a *real* issue. If it is, express it openly and honestly.

2. Identify the issue.

Very often, people feel anger without being able to identify its cause. Learn to uncover the source of your anger and to deal with your emotion as if it were a concrete object. Once you know what is causing your anger, you can work on its resolution.

3. Listen to the meaning behind the words.

Is your partner upset because you left the caps off the felt-tip markers, or is something else going on? Often you will have to listen carefully, "reading between the lines," to discover the origin of your partner's unhappiness. It may be just that your partner is in a bitchy mood, or there may really be something else going on. Ask questions, and if the real cause of anger is not clear, take the time to explore together what it could be.

4. Deal with anger as quickly as possible.

Some couples have agreements to reserve the expression of anger until privacy is possible, while others are comfortable showing their anger in public. Whether you choose privacy or public confrontation, deal with your anger quickly and completely and get it over with. Above all, don't hold a grudge or keep score. Remember, you are *both* on the same team and *each* of you is one-half of the partnership.

5. Keep on track.

Stick to the problem, don't dredge up old feelings or issues. Live in the present, but learn from the past. Avoid tactics that will obstruct your progress toward resolution, such as name-calling or verbal blows that you know will hit a sensitive nerve.

6. Put yourself in your partner's place.

It always helps to understand the other person's point of view. Because copreneurs are two people, there will be two views of every issue. When you learn to place yourself in your partner's position you will be better able to understand that other point of view. To resolve an issue, you must deal with all of its aspects. Understanding your partner will bring you closer together.

7. Fight fair.

A no-holds-barred approach to disagreements can be very destructive. Anger is often a moral emotion that can be used to right a wrong or correct an injustice. It is also a communication tool that can help you and your partner grow together. And it is not a contradiction in terms to acknowledge that anger can be expressed with kindness and consideration for your partner's feelings.

8. Don't be afraid to use humor.

When you see the absurdity of an argument, and feel the corners of your mouth itching to smile, give in to that urge and let it happen. *Shared* laughter is nature's finest balm to soothe frayed tempers. Interjecting humor during the heat of a disagreement can be a tricky business. But if it's sincere and not aimed at your partner, it's worth a try.

9. Learn from your mistakes and move on.

Experience is the best teacher. When you see that you've made a mistake, learn quickly from it, acknowledge it freely, and go on with the business at hand. Don't spend more time than necessary on *mea culpas*. Let go of past mistakes with the resolution not to repeat them again.

10. Never withdraw or build walls.

Withdrawing and building barriers can be used as an offensive as well as a defensive weapon. If you retreat into solitude, agreement and resolution with your partner will be impossible. Anger can be a spark for communication and enlightenment, but resolution requires the participation of both partners. Work at it together.

We find that most of our own arguments are not over big issues, and almost never over business, although often the tension created by business can serve as a catalyst for frustration, which can lead to disagreements. We have agreed *never* to air disagreements in front of a client, and rarely has our staff known when we were working through a sticky personal issue. Early in our relationship we made the decision to keep personal disagreements personal, and this style of dealing with conflict carried over quite naturally into our working relationship.

On occasion, we will find ourselves in a heated argument as we are driving over the Santa Cruz Mountains to attend a meeting with a client. Those tiffs can be quite silly, and our behavior absurdly comical. Our office on wheels, a Toyota van, becomes very small at those times and whoever is not driving will often crawl into the very last seat to sulk and gain space, ducking the other's eyes in the rearview mirror. However, it takes only a few minutes of sitting by yourself to feel ridiculous and to crawl back to the front seat.

No matter how serious or how trivial the argument, when the car stops and our feet hit the pavement of the client's parking lot, a transformation in our behavior toward one another always takes place. In spite of how angry or hurt we both might be, we set those feelings aside for the duration of our meeting. And neither of us can recall a time when we returned to the car and resumed an argument. In fact, more often than not, back in the car we can't even remember the original source of the disagreement.

Gradually, we have come to learn that arguments alone don't resolve problems; but they *can* lead to understanding the other's point of view, which is necessary to reaching a solution. It is what happens after the argument is over that is important. We both firmly believe that if you and your partner don't argue and disagree on occasion, you are not *really* communicating.

There may be times when a couple reach an impasse, finding it difficult or impossible to understand or accept each other's point of view. We are not advocates of protracted therapeutic counseling, which we feel can become self-serving and indulgent. Some therapists view anger as if it were a fixed bundle of energy, just waiting to burst out wherever it finds a weak spot. Like archaeologists they search continually for its roots, scratching away at the surface to unearth a new bone or shard. Although we don't feel it's necessary to dig and probe at relationships, we do recognize that occasionally an impartial professional third party, one who can step in to mediate and to assist in bringing two divergent viewpoints together, can be extremely helpful.

Therapy or counseling, we believe, should be problem-specific and discontinued as soon as the issue has been worked through. It can be especially useful to couples who are experiencing a deterioration in their communication and who need help to reestablish mutual understanding and reopen the lines of communication. It should be noted that we are not talking here about couples who are experiencing serious on-going distress in their relationship. They, of course, should seek appropriate counseling.

Irene Cohen strongly advocates that as part of their business plan, couples have a contingency plan for dealing with anger and impasses—a plan outlining how they will work together to solve any problems that arise in their working relationship.

There was a point where Sy and I were having a lot of arguments and problems over the business. We still argue a lot, but it's different than it was then. At that time, I said to Sy that I thought we needed a third party to mediate because we just couldn't agree.

So I called a psychologist in Manhattan and asked if he could see us. We went to him once and then again maybe six months later. Then the following year, when our daughter Diane joined the business, we were having problems adjusting to her. So the three of us went to discuss our problems with him.

We feel very strongly that a couple should have an outside source—a professional business consultant or psychologist who has dealt with business relationships, not someone who is just another business person, but one who will listen and allow you to work out your problem together. You need a person who will say, "You can work it out together if you talk to each other in a professional and businesslike manner, not dealing with it from an emotional standpoint." Even now, I will react to something Sy has said or done in an emotional way and I will say to myself, "Is this the way Stanley would have us deal with this problem?" We haven't talked to him for years, but who knows—we keep his number in our book just in case.

The Cohens have also worked out a mechanism in their business for establishing distance between themselves when needed. Irene pointed out that business has to move forward, even when one of the partners is unhappy with the other. In their company, Sy and Irene can always go to each other's assistant for information they need quickly to move their enterprise ahead. At those times when the couple is having communication problems they can still obtain information by not dealing directly with each other.

CRITICISM—A POWERFUL
COMMUNICATION TOOL FOR GROWTH

Like anger, criticism has both constructive and destructive potential. Both can be significant tools for effective communication and personal growth in any relationship. The reaction to criticism, its acceptance or rejection, depends upon two things —its delivery, and the ability of the recipient to perceive it as a positive rather than a negative message. We also believe that, as is the case with anger, a relationship in which there is no two-way criticism is one in which communication is incomplete.

In the early stages of a couple's working relationship, criticism appears often to be a source of friction. During the course of our interviews, many women discussed their discomfort at being criticized by their partners during the start-up phase of their enterprises. However, as their working relationships matured, their businesses became more solid, and the women grew more confident in their own roles and abilities, criticism evolved into a valuable tool for the growth of both partners.

When women in our culture are criticized, their response is often to internalize the critique, viewing it as a diminishment of their self-esteem. Males, on the other hand, seem much more comfortable accepting criticism as it relates to the specific action, project, or product under scrutiny. Perhaps this is because males have been acculturated to be competitive—and to succeed in competition they must be the best, continually learning, refining, and striving always to do better. Therefore criticism often plays a crucial and positive role in male development. There is, of course, a down side to competitiveness. The very nature of competition is stressful and causes distance between competitors, leading to isolation. Similarly, being noncompetitive in our society tends to place an individual on the sidelines as a noncontender, a position in which women often find themselves.

Copreneurs have learned the value of criticism in a safe, noncompetitive environment. Over time, both partners become comfortable receiving and giving constructive criticism. They understand that business is business, and that for criticism to be constructive it must not be given or taken personally.

When we first sat down to interview Donna and Harvey Clar, Harvey told us that he had been thinking about our meeting and there was one observation he wanted to make before we began our questions.

> If you're going to be in business together, things can't be personal— they've got to be business. I know that everybody's story is different, and that's what makes it exciting. But I'll bet all the couples you've interviewed said they were each other's best friend before they went into business together.
>
> If you're going to work together daily, and if you are going to put in the time that you have to for the business to be a success, you had better be each other's best friend. Because if you're not, then you're going to have too many problems and you won't be able to survive.
>
> You have to discuss things without those issues getting out of focus. If I criticize the way Donna is doing something, she can't take it as if it's a personal insult that she may be doing something wrong. And I can't take it personally if she thinks there's something I'm doing wrong. If you're best friends, then you can discuss things without making them personal. I think that's the one common denominator that's got to be there between entrepreneurial couples.

Like ourselves, Don and Audrey Wood collaborate creatively on the children's books they write and illustrate. Even on projects in which only one is under contract, the other plays a major, though outwardly invisible, role. Most authors and artists must work at their craft in isolation, and to receive honest appraisal or criticism many find it beneficial to join a writers' group or to cultivate a network of artistic peers. Since Audrey and Don work together as both artists and writers, they have become their own editorial and artistic critiquing committee of two. Before one of their books even arrives at the publisher, they believe it has undergone ten times more review than most other writers or artists are able to acquire from any peer group.

The advantage for Audrey and Don in reviewing and critiquing each other's work lies in the honesty and security that exist between them. Don observes that while others must work alone or in a critiquing group that is not as secure as their very intimate and trusting relationship, "We are able to express ourselves to each other quite strongly and not worry that we're going to burst the other person's ego. We can say exactly what we think and then the other takes it and uses what they find valuable."

Criticism plays a crucial role in the Woods' work style. And even though they work out of separate studios in their home, they have learned the value of *setting appointments* with one another to assure that sufficient time and concentration will be devoted during the critiquing process. Audrey notes,

> If the other person isn't being critical, then we assume they're just being lazy. We both want to take a part in each other's work in a positive as well as a negative way. Even when I'm working alone, on books that I'm both writing and illustrating, I bring Don in on the design stage; and he brings me into the designing phase on the books that he illustrates.
>
> At first it was a little disconcerting for publishers, because when they called or we would have a meeting, I would say, "Well, I'm bringing Don with me." And it must have appeared to them that I was bringing in reinforcements. I had to explain that, "This is the way we work—we work together. Even though I'm the one illustrating this book, he's still working with me in certain capacities, so he will be there to help make decisions." Now our publishers are used to this and when they call to set up a meeting with me, they'll ask, "Will Don be there too?"

Audrey and Don have learned the value of having two sets of ears and eyes at a meeting. They have discovered that while one is giving a presentation, the other is free to observe the reactions around them. Don told us of a "favorite trick" they employ during presentations.

> When I've been working on a piece of art for six or seven months of my life and I walk into a meeting to present it, my involvement in it is so great that I really don't see the reactions of others. I bring up the painting and say, "Well, here it is," and because of my intense emotional involvement, everything else is just a blur.
>
> Audrey has developed the habit of actually watching people to see if they're just verbalizing that they like it, or if their eyes expand and their jaws drop—all those reactions an artist *really* wants— instead of just saying, "Gosh Don, that's nice work."

So in these situations Audrey is doing something very important.

Because she doesn't have the emotional involvement in my work that I do, she can concentrate on what's going on—on the subtle and nonverbal communication that's so very important. We've learned that at those times when one of us has a crucial role and the other might be seen as just "a hanger-on," to have that "hanger-on" there is tremendously valuable.

To assure that criticism is a positive communication tool, one that contributes to understanding and growth, both partners need to establish trust in a noncompetitive environment. For criticism to be *constructive* rather than *destructive*, build it around the following guidelines.

1. Be specific.

When criticizing your partner, focus your comments only on that which requires attention. Avoid generalizations, phrasing your critique carefully to assure that only the issue at hand receives attention.

2. Be considerate.

Criticism should be a positive learning experience, not a vehicle for put-downs and sarcastic comments. And above all, be sensitive to your partner's feelings and the way your comments are being received. Keep your antennae out, and be ready to soften your approach if required.

3. Don't make threats.

If your criticism is couched as a personal threat, such as, "I just can't work with you if you don't change the way you're doing that!" your partner will focus on the threat to the relationship, rather than on the critique itself.

4. Separate the criticism from the individual.

Don't frame your criticism in terms of personal shortcomings or flaws. Be impersonal—deal with the issue separately from the individual. Your goal is not to belittle or humiliate your partner, but to help him or her grow.

5. Keep it light.

Even though your criticism has positive change as its goal, be sure to express it in terms that will not devastate your partner. Never be harsh or cruel.

6. Keep it short.

Make your observations and then move on. And always allow your partner time to digest your critique. If you beat your point to death, your relentless behavior will become the focus of your partner's attention, not the issue with which you wish to deal.

7. Deliver it promptly.

For criticism to be effective, it should coincide closely with your awareness that change is called for. Don't delay your comments, and above all, don't wait until you are angry to make your feelings known.

8. Never criticize your partner in public.

Unlike anger, which should be an equal interaction and may, if the partners agree, take place in the presence of others, criticism should always be reserved for a time when privacy is assured. Sometimes even the gentlest criticism, which would be taken well if delivered in private, will explode like a bomb if outsiders are present.

9. Keep your criticism in perspective.

Remember that in the long view of your relationship, issues that appeared monumental at the time they arose will often in hindsight be seen as the molehills they really were. View your partner as a whole person, recognizing that the part you are criticizing is really a very small portion of his or her total make-up.

10. Remember, criticism is an opportunity.

Criticism should be a positive experience for both partners. Growth and change should be the goals of every critique. Make criticism a positive part of your normal communication, and use it honestly to build and maintain the trust between you and your partner.

Although we have dealt here with anger and criticism primarily as valuable communication tools, praise is just as important for the growth of every individual, and should also be generously included in daily interactions. We once knew a manager who found it almost impossible to give praise. He felt that his task was to serve as critic, helping his subordinates to grow by pointing out every little mistake. Only the most outstanding performance was given positive recognition, and then with reluctance. Even when his workers knew they had done an outstanding job, they felt defensive and insecure when they presented their work for his approval. It is just as important for people to know when they are doing a job well as it is for them to know when improvement is needed. Use praise often, freely, and without hesitation.

PACTS AND AGREEMENTS

Some of the couples we talked with have negotiated pacts or agreements that relate either to their personal or working relationships. In our own case, from our first day together we have had a pact that our bed is a "nuclear free zone" where no arguing is allowed. In addition, we have agreed never to go to sleep angry. We have never broken those agreements—although we must admit that we have had a few long nights. At work we have many agreements; however, few have been formalized. But when it comes to anger and criticism, we have agreed to deal with those issues privately.

We ran across one particularly delightful contract, penned by Peter and Marina de Haydu, of Christine Valmy, during their honeymoon at the Hotel de la Mamounia, in Marrakech, Morocco. We found it so insightful that we have reproduced it here in its entirety.

LA MAMOUNIA CONTRACT

To establish the nature of our relationship with the aim of enhancing our love and our marriage.

Shall always share one bed.

Shall not permit outside interference or influence, including career, family, or children to disturb our relationship.

Maintain open communications, especially when hurt or angry.

Shall not allow stubbornness to jeopardize our happiness.

When the other person is hurt or angry, we should kiss and hug.

We should incorporate one another into each other's life.

Shall not forget to be tender.

All major decisions should be based on joint consultations.

Shall preserve Spirit of Adventure and not take ourselves too seriously or forget to be silly sometimes.

When pressure mounts—take a break.

Devote at least a half hour daily to speak with each other.

Bathe together at least once a month with an inspiring drink.

Devote to ourselves at least one full day a month.

Every year two weeks should be devoted to ourselves, away from family, children, and business.

Marina   Peter
Maracaibo, Venezuela
14 February 1983

A copy of this contract, which was handsomely calligraphied while the de Haydus resided in Venezuela, now hangs over the couple's bed in their Manhattan home. While this agreement was designed for their private life, and signed several years before they began working together, many of its points are especially useful in their working relationship. All either of them needs to do to invoke this agreement is to say "Mamounia Contract" and the other must abide by its terms. During arguments, when Peter or Marina sees that the other is hurt, invoking the contract brings an immediate halt to their argument and they must kiss and hug.

When we asked how they would reach a resolution if arguments could be immediately dropped, Peter replied that usually arguments don't require resolution because they are over trivial matters. Following that discussion with the de Haydus, the two of us began taking a closer look at the substance of our own disagreements, and we have come to realize that Peter and Marina are quite right—most of our own arguments are over topics that really don't matter and often require no resolution.

All the copreneurs we talked to stressed that anger and criticism should be dealt with directly, honestly, and as quickly as possible. These busy couples don't have time to deal with veiled anger—sulking, whining, or other manipulative behaviors —or with unkind, negative criticism.

Successful copreneurs are serious, mature individuals with little patience or time for game-playing. They relate to each other as equals, dealing with anger and criticism fairly and with compassion. For copreneurs, anger and criticism are two very important tools for effective communication. They recognize that criticism can be a constructive agent for growth, and that anger should be viewed as a warning light—it is one of life's significant markers that action is required.

CHAPTER

11

Dust Balls and
New Life Forms

As we approached the end of the previous chapter, we looked up at the clock to discover that it was three in the afternoon. Realizing why our stomachs were growling, we headed for the refrigerator. And there we found the title for this chapter. As we began foraging for food, digging into the the depths of the refrigerator, Frank groaned, "God, isn't there anything to eat—and what *was* this stuff anyway?"

Reaching for a blue pitcher that had contained orange juice the last time either of us looked, Frank stumbled upon another ghastly new life form. "Yecch! This stuff could kill you!" he exclaimed, grabbing the plastic bottle of dish soap—only to find it empty. Simultaneously we began tossing what *used* to be food out of the refrigerator into the trash container—liquefied lettuce, the carcass of a chicken, a carton of sour milk—everything except the perennial jars of mustard, mayonnaise, and ketchup. Standing back from the empty refrigerator, we knew it was time for another trip to the supermarket. "Well, since there's nothing edible here, would you like to take me out to lunch before we go to the market?" Sharan asked.

Our treks to the market are filled with the best of intentions. We lovingly select each vegetable and piece of fruit, stock up on salt-free lunch meats and cheeses, and religiously read the contents of every package, weeding out those with suspect and unpronounceable ingredients. And each time we restock the cupboards and pack the refrigerator with good healthy food, we rediscover the remnants of a previous foray, purchased weeks earlier, with expired pull dates and exotic furry growths threatening ptomaine or botulism.

Because of our busy schedule and our propensity to get lost in our work, much of the food we purchase in hopes of eating at home goes to waste before we have time to prepare it. Most meals are last-minute affairs—a dash to our favorite rosticceria for a roast chicken and twice-baked potatoes, a call to have pizza delivered, or, more frequently, taking a much-needed break by going out for a meal to one of several restaurants that have become our haunts. These days, a *real* meal at home, lovingly prepared, is an all-too-infrequent occurrence. In reaction to having wasted so much food in the past we have begun to purchase no more than one or two days' provisions at a time. While our altered buying habits have cut down on the waste, our cupboards are usually as bare as Mother Hubbard's.

It has long been known that dual-income families have transformed the heart of many American households—the kitchen—into lonely transit stations. Once the gleaming shrine of every home, for many busy families kitchens are now merely rooms where food is zapped in microwaves to be eaten on the run—and ours is no exception. Busy Americans are stocking up on greater quantities of microwaveable products, eating out more, and turning to gourmet delicatessens to help them cope with the demands of their lives.

Americans are not only changing the way they use their kitchens; because of the grueling schedules to which dual-income families must adhere, compromises are being made elsewhere in the house as well. Market research points to a growing trend of mounting dust balls and strange new life forms taking over households like pods from *The Invasion of the Body Snatchers.* Windows are a little less transparent, floors no longer have that "see yourself shine," and spring cleaning may not get done until fall—if at all. And despite the best efforts of marketeers hustling household cleaning products, sales have dropped five percent since 1985, while the use of maids and house-cleaning services is on the rise.

A fair number of the couples we encountered employ household help on a weekly basis, and a few enjoy the services of a live-in helper. However, a considerable number of couples maintain their residences without assistance, often sharing those responsibilities with their partner and their children.

Gayle and Joe Ortiz recognized from their own full schedule running Gayle's Bakery in Capitola, California, that working couples have little time to plan and prepare healthful and nutritious meals. Four years ago the couple opened their Rosticceria, a delicatessen adjacent to their French bakery, catering to their busy professional clientele by providing a tasteful menu of take-out meals. Gayle told us how they discovered the concept of the Rosticceria on their first trip to Italy.

> Driving through Tuscany, we began to see that there were shops where you could get wonderful, complete meals that you could take to your hotel or a park and eat these great roast chickens, pastas, rices, salads, and sandwiches. So when we returned home we began planning our deli, knowing that there was going to be space next to our bakery that would be available. We ordered the spit the chickens are roasted on from a company outside Florence, and they designed an oven shell for the space we would be moving into.
>
> Now that it's established, it's become such an integral part of our own lives and the lives of our customers as well. It's the completion of the bakery. It's part of our message, part of what we are offering people. The deli has evolved out of what our customers want from us. They want food that has been ready-made in our kitchen. They come in because we are baking and cooking in our kitchen and they don't have time to in theirs.

For fifteen years, Sy and Irene Cohen had a housekeeper who came in every day at around noon to manage their house, doing virtually everything from meal planning and shopping to supervising painters. In addition, she prepared their evening meal. Until her recent death, Irene sadly recalls,

> She ran the house. Beatrice took care of us and was simply wonderful—she was everything a working couple needs, a mother, wife and household manager, she was a true housekeeper in the old tradition. Right now we are in limbo. She just died of cancer and I don't know what I'm going to do. I have not the heart yet to look for someone else. She didn't sleep in, but came in the early afternoon and didn't leave until after we had finished our dinner.

The Cohens' decision to hire their housekeeper came at the suggestion of Sy's mother, who was visiting at a time when Sy was recuperating from a long hospitalization. As Irene told us,

> When Sy came home after being in the hospital for about a month, his mother came to see us. She called me at the office and volunteered to make something for dinner and I said, "Don't be silly, Mom, just grill something and put it on my plate." When I got home and we were eating supper, she asked what we did for dinner every night. When I told her that we usually ate out, her reply was, "That's not healthy, you're eating all the wrong things and that's bad for you. Why don't you get someone to come in?" I responded, "Not with two people, we don't need someone every day because we're never here." It was her idea that we hire a housekeeper to come in at one or two o'clock and stay until after our evening meal was finished. Now I'm in the personnel business, and here I was asking *her*, "How are we going to find that someone?" She just looked at me and said, "Why don't you put an ad in the classifieds?"
>
> Beatrice was the fiftieth person to apply and she was like a mother to us. Her being there made sure we got out of the office, went home, and had a healthy dinner. Since her death, we're working until seven or eight o'clock and don't have dinner until ten! But we've found a few restaurants that have come to know us. They know not to put bread on our table, that we don't need a drink before dinner, and when they prepare our foods, not to use fats and butter. They're used to our coming in regularly and because they've come to know our routine, they're not insulted that we don't order a full-course meal.

EASY LIVING AND PEACE OF MIND

While most of the couples we met live in traditional homes or condominiums, two copreneurs have located their combined enterprise and residence on farms. Two other couples maintain their homes in small trailers, and one couple, professional cross-country truck drivers, spend most of the year in motels or the cab of their truck.

We were surprised to discover these coentrepreneurs who have elected to radically simplify their lives at home, forsaking the American Dream of home ownership, at least for the present, to focus their attention and energies on their businesses and relationships. In fact, we believe it is not the high price of real estate alone that accounts for these couples who are shifting their priorities away from home ownership to other areas of personal importance—education, career changes, the establishment of a business, travel, or just the peace of mind that can come from having someone else worry about the plumbing, leaky roofs, and unexpected repairs. Some people view home ownership as just one more black hole that will absorb their time, energy, and financial resources.

When veterinarians Tom and Sharon Dose moved to Reno to establish their clinic, they decided to simplify their life by not replacing the large home they had sold in Las Vegas. Their humorous insight into what the maintenance of a large residence meant to them underscores that home ownership is no longer for everyone. We sat with the Doses on the overstuffed couches in the rear of their clinic where they spend so much of their time with their Doberman Pinscher, Murphy, as Tom amused us with his woeful tale of home ownership.

One of the priorities that everyone raised in America has is to own a house and have a backyard and all the outward amenities of success. I've yet to see anybody who's successful have the time to utilize those amenities—and they'll drain every free minute you have. If you aren't cutting the grass or fixing a broken window or doing some other mundane chore, you're paying the bills to keep the place in operation. You're worried about the neighbors down the street destroying your land values because they have fourteen cars in front of their house, and are doing auto repairs in their garage. Or your neighbor decides to cut his grass at six on Sunday morning, right under your bedroom window!

The house we owned in Las Vegas was nineteen hundred square feet and we didn't have a prayer of keeping that place livable. We didn't even go into some rooms for months. It was a beautiful family home, four bedrooms, two baths, a nice backyard with a big double garage—perfect for a workshop. And we were never there!

When we moved here, we just forgot all that old crapola. We rented our apartment and now if there's something wrong, I just call somebody to fix it. And if the neighbors are making too much noise, I tell the landlord and he takes care of them. For us, it's very peaceful, easy living. It's small, there's no painting to be done, there's no yard to keep up, and it just takes away all the outside stresses.

Clif and Beth Moore, professional photographers, happily live on the road, running their business out of their combined home and film-processing laboratory. For the past twelve years, the couple have found all they need and want in their thirty-two-foot fifth-wheeler. Using Overton, Nevada as their home base, Clif and Beth can be reached by leaving a message on the automated answering service they have established through the telephone company. When we first met with the Moores they were in Apache Junction, Arizona. And the last time we spoke with them, they were heading north to visit their daughter in Alaska for the summer—no doubt satisfying their passion to capture nature on film along the way.

Not long ago we met with copreneurs Randy and Pam Dougherty, who make their living as square dance callers, an entertainment career that takes them all over the world—Canada, Saudi Arabia, Sweden, England, the Caribbean, and Hawaii. In the spring, summer, and fall of 1988, Pam and Randy called dances in twenty-eight states, four Canadian provinces, and Saudi Arabia.

During the winter months the couple's travel schedule allows them a breather, and they return to their small trailer in Mesa, Arizona, where they are resident callers at the Mesa Regal RV Resort, calling nineteen dances each week. Randy estimates that he calls "four or five hundred dances in a year. And each dance is usually about two hours long."

As the square dance caller, Randy, who was a high school teacher for six years in Minnesota, is the "star" of the team. But it's Pam, as his manager, who is responsible for scheduling and keeping track of their incredibly complex globe-trotting itinerary, as well as maintaining all the records for their enterprise and running her own clogging dance program.

Until two years ago the Doughertys owned a home in Minnesota. But today Pam expresses her relief at not having to worry about maintaining a large residence.

> Right now, I feel like I don't even care if we never own a house again. Sometimes I walk into someone else's home and say, "Boy, would I like to have a house—this is really nice!" Yet I have no real desire to have a house right now. They're too hard to maintain. In Arizona, when we get off the road, we always promise, "No more restaurants." And I resolve to fix meals at home. I start out pretty good, then I start running out of time. First we run out of time to cook. And when we finally do find the time to make a meal, we discover that we haven't had time to shop, so there's nothing to cook anyway, and it's back to the restaurant.

Even in a mobile home with under four hundred square feet of living space, busy copreneurs can feel as if housework consumes all their spare time and energy. Pam has resolved to hire help this year to relieve her of the chores of housework and laundry, so she can gain time in her busy schedule for relaxation.

TAKING TIME FOR YOURSELF

As a copreneur, it is necessary to make peace with the reality that life will be full of compromises if everything that needs to be accomplished is going to get done. You can't reasonably expect to put in twelve to sixteen hours a day at work, prepare lavish meals, maintain a meticulous house and a gracious style of living, and still have time left over for personal relaxation, without some outside assistance. Coming to this realization is not always easy, especially for the women in copreneurial relationships. For Liz Thomas of Chalif Inc., this understanding came about when her son began to fall behind in his school work, for which Liz blamed herself.

> As a family, we went to see a psychologist to help Nicky. He was having academic problems at school, which I thought were all my fault—but they weren't. Nicky has since done a great turnaround, and has all of his priorities in order. He decided he didn't need any more counseling, but I thought it would be good for me to continue.
>
> I had not resolved my career versus my nurturing role at home. It was a real identity crisis and it had to do with my trying to be Superwife, Supermother, and Superexecutive, without any time left for me. It came at a time when we were understaffed and I was trying to do everything at work and at home. The therapy really helped, I needed someone to help me process what was going on and to get rid of some of my guilty feelings for not being perfect. I didn't have any time for *me*, and it was something I had to learn—that it's important for everybody else's welfare that I am able to take care of myself as well. No one else was putting the pressure on me to be perfect—I was doing it to myself!

Donna Clar schedules one day each week when she doesn't go in to the auction gallery to work. That day is set aside to take care of personal business, maintain the house, and have the time necessary to collect her wits. On that day, Donna still drives to the gallery to meet Harvey for lunch—a testimony to the couple's deep friendship. Harvey also has structured relaxation into his busy schedule by leaving the gallery every afternoon for a workout at handball, a sport in which he excels.

Susan and Barry Brooks, of Cookies from Home, maintain their sanity and youthful physiques by working out together every afternoon at their gym. Sharan asked Barry how they manage to keep so trim, always surrounded by their delicious cookies. He replied,

> We eat our cookies all the time and we can't be fat. Working out clears our minds and allows us to eat without gaining weight—and we love to eat, it's a passion for us.

Going to the gym together is the only way we both get there. It's not like we're playing tennis and having fun—we're usually doing aerobics or cycling. If we didn't go together, we'd each have all sorts of excuses not to exercise. Working out is a good physical and mental release for us.

Balancing the world of work with the demands at home is one of the greatest challenges that an entrepreneurial couple will encounter. It goes without saying that there are not enough hours in each day to accomplish all that needs to be done at work, let alone in a busy household.

The first hurdle to overcome is psychological. A couple must learn to compromise and set priorities on what has to be done, what someone else can do, and what they can live without doing. This is particularly difficult for entrepreneurial couples who are both driven to perfection, seeking to create the best for their enterprise, for their home, and for their family.

Women in particular have difficulty relinquishing control of the household and accepting compromises in the home. Couples dealing with organizational problems at home may well emerge as a major issue for the coming decade. Sam Edelman of Sam & Libby, California addressed this issue.

This is one of the most difficult areas for Libby and me in our relationship. I am unwilling to plan dinners—or at least in the past I've been unwilling—and because we are both so busy, I find Libby not wanting to plan them right now either. And yet when I say, "I'll take it over," she doesn't want me to. But she doesn't really want to do it either.

She says she doesn't want to be so structured, and that she's always been able to throw things together at the last minute and enjoys the spontaneity. But that spontaneity comes at a big cost. Shopping at the most expensive market at the last moment, rather than planning in advance and having the meals structured for the rest of the week, results in additional expense.

But when you consider the benefits of working together, should that extra expense be a real matter of importance in the life of an entrepreneurial couple? Right now, planning our meals in advance is just not part of what we're all about. After all, I'm not doing any meal planning either. We spend more money now on meals, but the payoff is that we are able to spend more productive time at the office. This give and take between what we *think* we should be doing and what we *are* doing is just part of our life today.

For Liz Thomas, the realization that her expectations to do everything were *only* hers was a significant discovery. And in our own life, while we have always shared the responsibilities of our household, we have also shared in the guilt when we've fallen behind and the house has gotten out of control. We've worked through that guilt now, realizing that we can't do everything. We do what can be done, when we can do it, and now accept that for the time being, our household is less organized than either of us would prefer.

If seeking outside help is your solution to maintaining your house, keeping dust balls and other life forms at bay, don't be discouraged if just the right person doesn't appear quickly. Remember, Beatrice was the fiftieth person the Cohens interviewed. And if you don't have time to cook healthy meals, you might launch a search for delicatessens with healthy ready-made food or restaurants that are willing to tailor meals to your dietary requirements. Small neighborhood restaurants often appreciate steady customers, and some are quite willing to go out of their way to please. After all, they too are entrepreneurs, and understand busy schedules all too well.

And don't forget the couples who have voluntarily simplified their lives, by living in apartments, trailers, and even a truck to bring about an ease of living and peace of mind. While apartment life or living on the road is not everybody's cup of tea, we can learn a lesson from the example of these copreneurs who have pared their possessions down to the essentials. *Voluntary simplicity* does not mean to do without, but to possess only what is truly important to you. Even while living in a large home, there are ways to benefit from simplification. Choose your possessions with care, since you will have to care for them.

In coping with our own household, we've made friends with our microwave, share responsibilities equally among all the occupants of the house, and have learned to accept that someone else's way may not be ours—but the job still gets done. We're learning to set aside time to relax and to do what we need to do for ourselves. And most important, we've learned not to feel guilty about what can't be done. Because time wasted on feelings of guilt is just that—a waste.

CHAPTER

12
The Family
Juggling Act

Copreneurs are coming to terms with the juggling act of balancing their families, their homes, their enterprises, and whatever time may be left over for a social life and personal interests. The entrepreneurial couples who appear in *Working Together* have a firm grip on the reins of their businesses, and the patterns of their personal lives are solidly established.

These twenty-five couples, who represent the first wave of pioneering copreneurs, are a mature group of individuals, and so are their enterprises, most of which are well past the critical start-up phase. Three-fourths of these couples have children, some from previous marriages. In forty percent of the couples at least one of the partners has been married before, and eighty percent of those couples formed blended families.

When the copreneurs we met embarked on their ventures, twenty percent did so with infant children in tow. Today, while nearly half of the families have children living at home, only four have pre-school-age children. Two of those four couples are involved in start-up businesses. Six of the couples, or twenty-

four percent, have decided not to have or to postpone having
children.

Our own blended family has reached that stage where our
offspring are gaining independence, with the two older children
away at college and only the youngest, at sixteen, remaining in
the nest. When we started our agency, however, all three,
Frank's two sons and Sharan's daughter, were living at home, in
addition to our German exchange student, Alex Kusch. During
that time our enterprise permeated our lives, taking precedence
over all but the most pressing family commitments. For the first
two years, we were consumed by a frenzy of activities that kept
us on the run from dawn until late into every evening, six or
seven days a week—meetings with clients, designers, and
printers, as well as hours of writing at the computer, planning
campaigns, and plodding through the tedious administrative
tasks that are so much a part of every business.

Fortunately, our children were old enough to fend for themselves, and often for us as well, pitching in to clean the house,
do the laundry, and occasionally prepare a meal. They watched
the progress of our enterprise with interest, discussing clients,
admiring our creations, and not infrequently critiquing our
work. When we found ourselves in a time crunch on a project
they would all lend a hand, assembling marketing materials and
stuffing envelopes. And when it came time to transcribe the
tapes from our interviews for this book, our two oldest children
sat at the computers for weeks, during their summer breaks
from college, transcribing taped interviews into thousands of
pages of conversations with copreneurs.

Our children, like the offspring of so many other entrepreneurial couples, see first-hand what is involved in starting and
running an enterprise. Theirs is not a romanticized notion of
owning your own business—they know all too well the meaning
of "sweat equity." Since our three children are still students,
they are only occasionally employed by our agency. However, a
quarter of the copreneurs we interviewed reported that their
adult children hold full-time positions in their companies, often
with management responsibilities.

Sy and Irene Cohen's daughter Diane began as the management information systems director, coordinating all of the com-

puter systems for the entire company and is now president of
the personnel division. Three of Ted and Joyce Rice's five children are employed by T.J. Cinnamons—one as director of Canadian operations, another as manager of franchise services, and
the third as regional franchise field manager. And the only child
of their partner, Ken Hill, is employed by T.J. Cinnamons as
manager of the warehouse.

Donna and Harvey Clar's youngest son Danny has worked in
their auction gallery since he was eleven. Today he is an essential part of the business, taking turns with Harvey on the
auction block as the auctioneer. During their auctions the father
and son each work an hour on and an hour off, allowing
Harvey to mingle with the crowd. Harvey told us,

> It gives me a chance to relax, walk around, and talk to some of the
> people. Most of our clientele have seen Danny grow up. He's always
> been around and they'll tell us, "God, I remember Danny when he
> was just a little boy playing around the gallery." Now they see his
> son, who is only eight months old and when they come in they say
> to me, "Isn't this great? There's Harvey, Donna, Danny, and his
> little boy. And look, Danny is auctioning. When I came in and
> heard the voice, Harv, I thought *you* were on the block, but it's
> Danny—you sound exactly the same!" The feeling that this is a
> secure business with a secure family behind it makes it seem like it's
> going on forever and that appeals to our customers.

Liz Thomas of Chalif Inc. cannot stress too strongly the
influence their enterprise has had on their four children, all of
whom work in the business, two as full-time employees.

> I think starting this company has probably been more valuable to
> our children than any other education could have been. They have
> really known every aspect of the business—they've seen how the
> company has grown, they've been privy to all the financial situa-
> tions and everything that's happened to us. We've always been very
> open concerning our business, and as a result they've become very
> astute.
> And, most important, they've learned at a very early age that you
> can feel as if the world has fallen on your head and the bottom has
> dropped out, and that it is still possible to dig your heels in and
> turn that failure into an opportunity without taking drugs, getting
> divorced, or all the "usual" methods of dealing with catastrophe.

And I think that's probably been as valuable as anything that's ever happened in all our lives.

Tucked away in historic Sag Harbor, New York, located on the tip of Long Island, is the combined woodcarving studio and residence of Bob and Fran Hand. Sag Harbor is Bob's lifelong home; before he became a master woodcarver of waterfowl, birds of prey, and songbirds he was a potato farmer on the farm that had been in his family for generations. The location of the Hands' studio is ideal since Sag Harbor is the year-round home for many species of birds and a stopover for migrating waterfowl.

Since Bob, an avid hunter, was old enough to hold a whittling knife he has carved utilitarian hunting decoys. After his father and grandfather died within three weeks of each other, Bob attempted to carry on the family farm alone. However, the farm was more than he could handle by himself, and he changed careers. Working as a furniture restorer, Bob continued to carve more and more intricate decoys as a hobby. Customers who came into his shop with furniture to be repaired soon discovered his woodcarvings. Bob recalls that the first bird he sold went for $175. "That was big time! I never touched another chair—I just made up my mind then and there that this was what I was going to do."

Bob's hobby quickly became a full-time artistic career, which he has now pursued for over fifteen years. He is recognized as a world-champion woodcarver, and his work can be found in the finest private collections throughout the country. His beautiful decorative decoys can fool the eye into believing they are living creatures, and today his work commands prices as high as thirty-five hundred dollars.

When Bob and Fran married six years ago, Fran began woodcarving and is becoming an artist in her own right, creating intricately detailed shorebirds. In addition, the couple work together on many decorative decoys, with Fran using an electric burning tool to etch each feather, creating texture and realism on a bird that her husband has fashioned out of Louisiana tupelo gum or white cedar from New Jersey. Each bird requires more than a hundred hours of painstaking carving, detailing, and painting before both of the Hands are satisfied with its perfection.

As we talked with the couple, we watched with admiration as Bob meticulously painted the detailed feathers of his nearly completed brant waterfowl while his eldest son Bobby worked nearby on one of his own decorative decoys. Two weeks later, father and son both won awards with those uncannily lifelike creations at The World Show, an international competition held at Ocean City, Maryland, where nearly a thousand artists had entered over two thousand decoys. Bob's brant placed first in its division, and Bobby received two awards—an honorable mention for his gadwall waterfowl and a blue ribbon in the intermediate division for his exquisite carving of an old-squaw drake.

Bobby, now twenty-two, has carved at his father's side in their Sag Harbor studio since he was eleven. His younger brother Tommy has also carved but today is more interested in sports. "He's got plenty of artistic talent," his father told us proudly, "but he's into baseball and basketball and he just can't sit still long enough to carve."

Our son Elliott joined us during our interview with the Hands. Visiting with the woodcarvers provided a rare opportunity for him to witness first-hand the artistic apprenticeship of someone close to his own age. The two young men spoke quietly together at Bobby's workbench as we interviewed Bob and Fran. On the ferry back to New London, Connecticut, Elliott expressed his admiration for Bobby's talent, his knowledge, and his unique opportunity to learn from his father, a master woodcarver.

True apprenticeships, like those that were so prevalent among the craftsmen and artists of the Renaissance, are rare today. Stepping into the Hands' workshop, where Bob is nurturing the talents of his wife and son, was like being transported back to a time when families worked together, passing skills and knowledge from generation to generation. For the Hands, working closely together enhances not only Fran's and Bobby's abilities; it is part of an interactive process that is resulting in the artistic and professional growth of all three carvers. The respect Bobby holds for his father is readily apparent.

> Can you imagine that for fifteen years my father has been doing this? I have trouble knowing when the bird's done. Because I've been working on it for so long, I don't know when to stop putting paint on it. It's very frustrating when you have a picture in your head and you know what you want it to look like, but your ability doesn't match that or you just don't have time. That's what makes me want to go out and get a job somewhere else sometimes. There are so many details you could include on a bird, you could spend forever on one.

But the elder Hand, who has judged many competitions and has an unfailing eye for perfection and talent, knows that his son may one day surpass his own abilities. "He's a good artist and has a lot of natural ability," Bob says, describing his son's talent and the way the family works together in their studio.

> It's not that easy to work with me. I don't hold back, you know—I'm a pusher. We all sit here critiquing each others' birds. I'll see something and Fran will see something else. And Bobby will see something the two of us missed altogether. I'll tell you, working closely like this definitely improves the quality of each of our work.
>
> With Fran helping me, I can produce more birds and I try to make each one better than the last. Since nobody taught me, I had to teach myself. I developed different techniques as I went along. We all keep finding new ways to carve and paint, and are continually discovering new techniques and little tricks. And the three of us benefit from the experimenting and learning that we all do. There's no end to what we can learn from each other.

Children of copreneurs are likely to be more knowledgeable and involved in the enterprises of their parents than are the offspring of either entrepreneurs or employees of another's business. These children are exposed to their parents' business over the breakfast and dinner tables, often joining them during business functions and social events. And since copreneurial enterprises frequently begin in the home, children don't become isolated from their parents' venture. In coast-to-coast discussions with copreneurs, a picture emerged of strong families, with parents who like and respect their children and enjoy their company, and with children who reciprocate their parents' display of affection, admiration, and respect.

TIME OUT AND TIME OFF

For most copreneurs, finding the time to socialize or just get away from their business can present a real problem. Because of the extremely close nature of their personal relationships, some couples seem not to seek out or to miss the company of friends. Many entrepreneurial couples have learned to balance their busy professional lives with a rich social calendar, while others clearly long for the time when the demands of their enterprise will diminish and allow them to resume an active social life.

Sam Edelman of Sam & Libby, California expressed his longing for the social activities that have been interrupted by their fashion shoe venture.

> We are a very social couple and love entertaining at home. But for the last year, our social life has been nonexistent. Any socializing we do today revolves only around the business. The *house* has house guests, but that is because we feel more comfortable with our business associates here than in a hotel. But I really miss the social life—I miss it a lot. I think I miss it more than Libby does. Sam & Libby is our life today—this entrepreneurial venture is everything. Fortunately, our kids can go everyplace with us and we take them everywhere. Our children are important and we don't want to miss being with them. But our social life? It's on hold.

More than a few of the couples interviewed echoed Sam's lament over the loss of their social activities. However, as we met with couples whose businesses were more mature we discovered that rich social interactions and copreneuring *can* co-exist. For Donna and Harvey Clar, socializing is just that—purely social. "We do very little entertaining as part of the business," Donna stressed.

> I would say that the only socializing we do in the business occurs when we simply can't get out of it. If we have a choice, our social life is separate from the auction gallery. We're out a lot. We have

many good friends and we enjoy them immensely. Harvey and I couldn't live without our friends.

As much as we enjoy the business, we enjoy getting away from it and having an evening where the conversation has nothing to do with work. I think that airs out your mind so that when you get back to the office you can think a little more rationally. You can work out a problem you've had, saying, "Well, that wasn't so bad," because you got away from it. And you can only step away from the business by discussing other things and exploring new topics, whatever they might be. If you work all the time, you get stale.

Some copreneurs enjoy socializing with friends who are also involved in their own enterprises and can therefore appreciate the pressures and time constraints that running a business place on a couple. Susan and Barry Brooks of Cookies From Home frequently spend time with other entrepreneurial couples, finding the interchange of ideas and the sharing of solutions to problems they all encounter to be beneficial. As Susan says,

> We can creatively help and support each other. Working together is a unique experience and many times sharing our experiences with other couples who have had similar problems is very valuable. We meet with these other couples on a regular basis, and when we get together we have a great time.

Veterinarians Tom and Sharon Dose find it difficult to leave their animal patients or the clinic to spend time with friends. Their solution has been to nurture a friendship with a couple who run a business in Reno that grooms and boards animals. Sharon explained that because their friends work together in a business centered around animals, they understand the demands of the Doses' veterinary practice and the reasons behind their inability to schedule social events in advance.

> Our relationship with them is very relaxed. If things work out for them and for us so that we can all do something together, it's usually planned on the spur of the moment. We might pack a picnic, drive into the hills, and just sit and relax together, or we'll just call and ask if they would like to get together to watch a video.
>
> They work as hard as we do. And anybody who works with animals knows they are constantly pooping and peeing and barking and can drive you nuts. So we all can sympathize with each

other. People who work with animals are really boring to people who don't, and the four of us are always talking about animals. It's like sitting around with mothers who talk about nothing but their kids—and I don't get a big bang out of that because I'm not into kids.

One of the things our friends bring to our relationship is to get us away from home or the clinic. In our free time, if it's just the two of us, we won't go out, we'll just sit here and relax together. They have really helped us to get away when we've needed to. They contribute to our life, we talk about everything and we'd be kind of hard up for companionship without them. There are very few folks who understand the stresses of a husband and wife team working together.

Don and Audrey Wood, children's book authors and illustrators, socialize with family and close friends, and they also enlist their help during the initial phases of working on each new book. The couple produce a script of the story, provide costumes and makeup, and everyone joins in, acting out the story while Don sketches and takes photographs from which to work. As Audrey describes the scene,

It's like a dramatic production. We cast our characters, which are usually based on friends, neighbors, and family. Each book has part of us in it. The Victorian house in *The Napping House* is actually our house, and I'm the mother in *Heckedy Peg* and the children in that story are my nieces, nephews, and neighborhood kids. Our son Bruce has been used as a model more than anyone, although he's outgrown the age of the characters in our stories— we'll have to do a story with a handsome young prince!

We produce these little plays right here in the living room before Don gets to the point of illustrating them. We tell stories with pictures and these productions help us add to the drama of our books. It's a wonderful way for us to work together and it's a wonderful way to include our family, friends, and neighbors in our work as well.

It's really one of the highlights of our creative process, and our friends and family are very proud of the role they play in our books, particularly since each one of them is really quite recognizable in the finished art. Just before the art is sent off to our publisher, we have a showing of everything we've been doing and everyone in the book is there, along with all our family members. This event is very important to us because it celebrates our reentry into the world of

family and friends, which we have to leave behind for the two or
three final months of every book.

While finding the time to socialize can be a challenge for
many copreneurs, structuring vacations into busy schedules
sometimes presents an even greater dilemma. In any business,
the day-to-day operation makes breaking away very difficult;
but for some copreneurs, leaving the business behind, even for a
few days, can prove to be an outright impossibility.

Because the two founders cover so many responsibilities in a
coentrepreneurial business, their absence often brings business
to a standstill—and few enterprises can afford even a temporary
halt in cash flow. Ian Weinschel, of River Bank, Inc., underscored this point as he discussed how he and Betsy incorporate
their four children into their busy life as political media consultants by creating opportunities for the family to travel together.

Whenever you run a business yourself there is the realization that
you can't go home at five o'clock and say "We'll leave it for someone
else," or "We'll take care of it later." Betsy and I are constantly on
call and it's like having a rocket in the air—if you stop the thrust it
falls to earth and you are out of business.

When we must travel we try to bring our children along with us.
Two years ago when we worked on the California senate race, we
put all the kids in the car to scout shooting locations, and we had a
great time doing it. We drove the coastline and discovered Muir
Woods, which became a symbol of the campaign and was featured
in our commercials showing the candidate walking through the
redwoods with *his* family.

We were able to bring the children, share the experience with
them, and tie it all back into our work. I think one of the reasons
we were so successful with that campaign had nothing to do with
politics, but was the feeling of family that we were able to capture
on camera for our candidate. When people watch political commercials they are looking at the candidate's perspective on life and
how it matches their own and those commercials were an extension
of what *our* family discovered in California.

The kids are partners in the business. We ask their opinions and
there are a lot of times when their suggestions contribute to our
work. Whenever one of our candidates announces their candidacy,
we always try to bring the kids so they can feel a part of it. We take

them to the victory party and sometimes to the defeat party, if that's the outcome. Political campaigns are very exciting, and we feel there's a parallel between politics and life on our farm. Our kids see things being born and they see things dying, it's a natural process of every part of life.

Our lifestyle tends to break down the isolation that exists in other families. Our family has become the "group" and now it's the family versus the world, rather than just the two of us.

Although getting away on vacations with the entire family is difficult for the Weinschels during election years, they often include their children when they must be away from home. If Ian or Betsy is required at the editing facilities in New York, they will take one of their children along for companionship and to afford that child an opportunity to gain a broader sense of the world away from the farm.

Entrepreneurial couples make the most of any business trip, often scheduling time for relaxation into their itinerary. Therapists Ruth McClendon and Les Kadis travel throughout the world, conducting workshops for professionals on their family therapy techniques. But even when they aren't conducting the workshop together, the couple always travel together. Ruth explains,

> One of the things we've determined is that it's not worth traveling alone. I used to be in Europe alone ten days each month teaching and training, and it was awful! Now, if I'm conducting a workshop, Les is always there.
>
> When we were in Peru I did a radio program and all the material was mine, Les had no input in the program. However, I wouldn't have gone to Peru without him. We combine the travel for workshops with time off for relaxation. We've been to practically every country in Western Europe at least once or twice, and our trip to Peru was a combination vacation, volunteer medical mission for Les, and the radio program for me. I can't even remember when we've taken a vacation that was purely for pleasure—we usually combine business with time off.

Suzanne and David Brown of Plantation Farm Camp, also build "time out" into their business travel. Whenever they are away on business they make a date with themselves to visit a museum, go to the theater, or take the opportunity to see the sights—and they have made it a rule never to break that date.

When we embarked on our cross-country journey to interview couples for *Working Together*, we decided to travel by train. This leisurely form of transportation allowed us time to rest, work on other projects, explore the information we were gaining from the interviews, and experience just how enormous and diverse America really is. And since our trip coincided with our son Elliott's spring break, we arranged for him to fly to Providence, Rhode Island where we were meeting with restaurateurs Johanne Killeen and George Germon, and to continue on with us for the rest of our trip. During that same trip we were also able to visit our older son Anthony, who attends Swarthmore College near Philadelphia.

Even when Susan and Barry Brooks are on a family vacation, they find themselves promoting Cookies From Home. "Last year, Susan and I and the kids went to San Diego for a week in August," Barry told us, giving an example of how they combine family vacations with their business.

> Even though it was a family vacation with all four of us, Susan and I took a few days of that time to call on some of our corporate accounts there. I don't remember that we called the office every day, but we certainly touched base to have fresh cookies flown to the airport before we met with clients. This year we're planning to get away for three weeks. That's something we've never done before. We've never had more than one week at a time away from the company in seven years.

When the topic of vacations arose during our interviews, most of the copreneurs expressed the desire to be able to get away from the business on *real* vacations. Out of necessity, they have learned to take advantage of every opportunity for time off, and even include their children in their business traveling plans to maximize family time together.

It is characteristic of entrepreneurial couples to constantly refine and expand their enterprises. This continual state of change and growth makes it perpetually difficult for some couples to make the break from their businesses. When we asked Irene and Sy Cohen about the role vacations play in their lives, Irene responded,

> You want to start a fight, right? We don't get away often enough. I'd like to have a dollar for every vacation plan we broke. We can't leave because every time we get the business to a point where we can take off, we come up with the idea for another division and we're stuck at work again. But as long as we can travel together, we call it a vacation, even though it's work.

INVESTING IN THE COMMUNITY

We were impressed by the number of copreneurs we met who are actively involved in reinvesting the goodwill they have received from their customers back into their communities. We had not anticipated a pattern of community engagement among the copreneurs we interviewed. However, as we met couple after couple we learned that these people are committed to building not only a better business but a better community as well. Many are involved in civic, charitable, and educational projects, serving on advisory boards and committees and organizing community events.

Both Sy and Irene Cohen work actively in private and public organizations in New York City, and Irene outlined some of the programs in which they are involved.

> Sy does more charity work, with organizations like the Cerebral Palsy Foundation or the Board of Trustees for our temple, while I do community work that's related to our business.
>
> I've chosen to become involved in a lot of business-related community service work because that has an impact on the quality of our product—our product is employable people. If the school system in New York is bad and continues to be bad, our product will deteriorate. So I've put a lot of time and effort into such things as working with the Chamber of Commerce and with the public schools.
>
> Sy and I have given scholarships to high school students. And because we felt a need to do more, we're in the Join-A-School Program where we adopt schools and do everything we can to

bring students into a business environment, showing them the full range of job opportunities in our computer and telling them what companies are really like. We talk to them and tell them how the things they learn in school relate to the world of work. We help them to see why it is so important to stay in school.

Brian and Mary Harvey of Rakestraw Books have become cultural leaders in Danville, California. In addition to their active social life with a close group of friends, the Harveys have been instrumental in rallying their community around cultural events.

Danville is a distant suburb of San Francisco, and when the Harveys arrived there from Southern California they missed the theater, music, and other cultural activities that had been readily accessible in the Los Angeles area. Brian recalls,

We started spontaneously, organizing a bus load of people for a picnic to see Christo's Running Fence in Marin County. From that excursion, we began regular trips with season tickets to the Berkeley Repertory Theatre, the Oakland Symphony, and the San Francisco Opera. It was Mary who began this enterprise, and we called it Rakestraw Friendly. Those bus trips, with thirty-six participants for each event, continued for a few years until gas prices got to be horribly expensive.

Nine years ago, Rakestraw Friendly evolved into Rakestraw and Friends, a nonprofit corporation with the purpose of promoting music in Danville. This year, we're expanding the program to include jazz as well as chamber music. We have two hundred and fifty members and are now drawing world-renowned performers. The Woody Herman Band was just here.

We see our role as more than just booksellers. Our community involvement is the kind of activity that makes running the bookstore truly enriching. We're really proud to have been instrumental in forming this organization, and it's that kind of activity that allows us and our bookstore to give back to our customers, our friends, and our community all that we have received from them.

Susan and Barry Brooks are two strong individuals who believe that too many people feel that "life happens to them," that they are not in control. The Brooks are very much in control, and that means being actively engaged in all aspects of their community. The couple will rarely turn down a solicitation for their delicious cookies from any charitable organization or fund-raising event—from public television to the Phoenix Children's Hospital, you'll find Cookies From Home.

The dynamic couple also devote considerable energy to civic activities in their city and state, as well as actively participating in educational and professional organizations. Susan in particular is committed to organizations that assist women to find their way in the business world.

Not long ago we attended a community fund-raising event for a program to provide meals to those confined to their homes. Hundreds of friends and supporters packed the Capitola Theater to watch *La Femme du Boulanger (The Baker's Wife)*, and to enjoy food provided by the organizers, Joe and Gayle Ortiz of Gayle's Bakery. That evening, Joe presented a check for $2552 to the director of Meals on Wheels, representing 510 meals for the homebound recipients of the program.

The energy that copreneurs regularly invest in their enterprise often spills over into the community when their venture no longer requires their undivided attention. These couples, who have become accustomed to devoting so much of themselves to moving their business forward, often focus a portion of their considerable vitality outside their business, to the benefit of their community.

Copreneuring is the only way we know to integrate our work, our family, our friends, and our community into a harmonious whole. To us, it seems much more natural to work together in an enterprise of our own creation than to work separately in jobs that isolate us from each other as well as from our family, friends, and community.

Today, Americans work harder and longer than ever, and have less time for enjoyment in their lives. In 1973 the average American worked 40.6 hours each week. By 1985 the work week had expanded to 47.3 hours, an increase of over sixteen percent! And our leisure time has decreased by over thirty-eight percent, from 26.2 hours a week in 1973 to 16.2 hours in 1987. In *Time Wars: The Primary Conflict in Human History* (Henry Holt and Company, 1987), Jeremy Rifkin addresses this issue head-on. "We rarely have a moment to spare. Leisure time, once a mainstay of human life, is now a luxury. Compared to almost every other period in history, we seem to have less time for ourselves and far less time for each other."

For most copreneurs there are no boundaries between work and home or work and pleasure. Copreneuring offers challenges that are at the same time very rewarding and very demanding—and the most challenging of all is to learn how to integrate all aspects of your life while simultaneously moving your business forward with the most important person in your life.

PART FOUR

Copreneuring Is The Future

Copreneurs are not empire builders—they are dream builders, molding their personal and working worlds into their own unique visions.

CHAPTER

13

Copreneurs and the Business Community— New Partnerships for the Future

U nderstanding between individuals and growth in a relationship come from seeing all sides of a person; when some of those facets are not fully revealed, the relationship will take longer to mature. The copreneurs in *Working Together* have seized the opportunity to merge all the significant facets of their lives into a harmonious whole—their personal relationships, their worlds of work, and the universe of their families. Couples who do not work together have a life apart from each other that can never be fully shared or understood between them. At the end of the day, when they return home to common ground, these couples relate an *edited* tale of their day's events, often highlighting their successes or expunging their failures.

At the end of their day, couples who work together have shared the good and the bad, the successes and the failures— and their relationship grows stronger and matures faster as a result of those mutually shared experiences. While the couples in this book come from diverse backgrounds and enterprises, they all share common values. Copreneuring is really about friendships, relationships, shared commitments and goals, and the blending of the work and personal worlds into one integrated realm.

If we have an axe to grind, it is to make the business community aware of the resources that couples can bring to an enterprise, whether as co-owners or coemployees. It is time for the American business community to revive its social contract with its employees and to include couples working together in that agreement.

The 1980s saw workers taking control of their own lives, venturing out to form entrepreneurial enterprises in response to repeated violations of a social contract between big business and its employees. The landscape of American business is strewn with decades of broken promises. Promises of job security, the right to privacy, fully vested retirement, and health benefits are now viewed, during these difficult times of mergers, cutbacks, and shutdowns, as expendable by new management and ownership with commitments only to balance sheets.

We believe that the 1990s will usher in a return to values that have long been absent in the American workplace, values centered on the family as an independent economic unit. The business community should not only look closely and seriously at copreneuring as a model for management; it should also move to incorporate working couples into their organizations.

When Sam and Libby Edelman were turned down by venture capitalists they were shocked to find out that one of the reasons for their rejection was that they were an entrepreneurial couple and therefore not considered a good risk. Like all other coentrepreneurs, the Edelmans know that when couples work together their focus is on success. To copreneurs, one plus one is never two—it is the sum of each individual's talents, resources, energies, and commitment to their joint venture, plus the synergism between them. To couples who work together, one plus one is always three!

The bias of the venture capital community against entrepreneurial couples also exists in the broader business world, and is reflected in company policies designed to keep couples from working together as employees. Regrettably, very few companies in the business community today recognize that when couples work together as employees they often bring higher levels of communication as well as shared goals and commitments to company objectives and thus benefit the overall organization.

The business community is gradually coming to recognize that the bottom line can be affected positively when employees are given the opportunity to express and meet the often conflicting needs of all the roles in their lives—the roles of worker, spouse, parent, and even child as their own parents grow older and place increasing demands on their time. Management policies that allow employees to juggle the demands of family and work with greater ease, including flex time and job sharing, are indications that employees are increasingly being recognized as more than just workers and that their personal lives have an impact on their work lives.

We discovered one sector of the business community that is already reaping the positive benefits of couples working together and is now actively recruiting husband-and-wife teams. The trucking industry, which has always been a bastion of male dominance, has undergone a dramatic transformation since its deregulation in 1980. From the very design of the trucks to the architecture and operation of truck stops, this industry is feeling the effects of, and benefiting from, the inclusion of women into the ranks of drivers. On America's highways today there are perhaps nine thousand women behind the wheels of the heaviest rigs, and the vast majority of these women are half of a husband-and-wife driving team.

We contacted Mayflower Transit, Inc., in Indianapolis, Indiana, one of the top van lines in America, because we had heard that husbands and wives who own their own trucks often contract their services to the moving company. After a few telephone calls to Mayflower's headquarters, Frank was put in contact with traffic manager Eric Anders, who schedules and directs the busy itineraries of the van line's large pool of drivers.

Eric became very excited when we told him that we were doing research for a book about couples working together as coentrepreneurs. The reason for his enthusiasm became obvious as we learned more about the Mayflower operation and how it is benefiting from contracting with husband-and-wife driving teams. As we talked to Eric and pored over company literature, it became clear that Mayflower is an innovative company that is actively recruiting the participation of husbands and wives. But it was not always that way, Eric told us.

Prior to deregulation in 1980, we would accept a woman on a truck, but it wasn't encouraged as it was seen as taking the space of a male codriver. In 1980, Mayflower had less than two dozen couples on the road. But in the next two years the company quickly realized the value of couples and actually began an aggressive recruiting program to solicit them. We utilized drivers to spread the word at truck stops and focused on couples in recruiting meetings. Today, twenty percent of our total fleet is operated and managed by couples.

All this came about because management became aware that many of our customers preferred having couples move their furnishings. Shippers began to request them and Mayflower discovered that having a wife on the truck resulted in the team taking better care of the customer's possessions. With these teams, there seemed to be dramatic reduction in claims for damages, possibly because of the care taken by the wives in really inspecting the furniture for preexisting damage before it went on the trucks. The female drivers identified with "Mrs. Customer," making sure an extra wrap went on something fragile, and it took the pressure and stress off the client to have a woman involved in the move.

In addition, when husbands and wives are on the road we can schedule them for longer periods of time since they remain content because they are working together. We try to bring drivers whose spouses stay at home back every thirty days. But most couples can stay out for as long as three months and that means more revenue for Mayflower and more profit for our owner/operators.

There's also improved productivity in having a couple on the truck. Drivers are able to reduce their overhead because the female partner now actually helps in loading the trailer. Prior to the 1980s, you would rarely have seen a woman lifting a chest of drawers. Today, they're sharing in all the workload, from driving to loading to keeping the records and log books. They truly are half of the business, and our owner/operators are exactly that—small independent businesses working for us on a contract basis.

Every month Mayflower selects a Driver of the Month from each division based on safety and claims records, among other criteria. Those drivers are then considered for the honor of

Driver of the Year in their division. David and Nancy Laffen of Novato, California were the 1987 Household Goods Drivers of the Year. They have been married for two years, and during that period they have worked together as owner/operators of their own moving van, contracting their services to Mayflower.

David, who had been a partner with his father in a bicycle shop in San Diego, California, purchased his first truck in 1982 and has since established himself as one of Mayflower's premier van operators. He recalls the reaction of his dispatcher when he announced his wedding plans.

When I told Eric Anders that I was going to get married, his first reaction was, "Oh, don't do that," because he thought Nancy would be at home and I'd soon be out of the business—I could see it written all over his face. But when I mentioned that she was going to be my partner, it was like the sun came out again. You could just see from Eric's expression his tremendous sense of relief because he knew that when couples work together as partners in our industry it's good for both the company and the marriage.

After months of trying to coordinate our busy schedule with the Laffens' equally complicated cross-country itinerary, we finally caught up with David and Nancy in Concord, California where Eric had been able to schedule an evening during which we could interview them.

The Laffens had spent the day loading household furnishings into their forty-eight-foot trailer for transport to New York City. They had skillfully packed the van from bottom to top and front to back, including a grand piano and a shiny new BMW automobile. We watched in awe as David adroitly maneuvered sixty-five feet of tractor and trailer through the parking lot of the shopping center where we had arranged to meet.

The rig was absolutely beautiful, from its glistening chrome wheels and quadruple gas tanks, which give it a range of 2500 miles between fuel stops, to the sparkling running lights that mark the top of the enormous thirteen-foot-high trailer. Before the couple had even stepped down from the tall cab of their truck, we could see their pride in their profession and commitment to excellence from the polished condition of their metallic green tractor and trailer with the familiar Mayflower ship and name on its sides.

When we were face to face with the Laffens, standing in front of their rig introducing ourselves, we were immediately struck by how young, physically fit, and attractive they both are. In fact, David looks more like the national bicycle racing champion he used to be than like the stereotype of a burly truck driver.

David and Nancy own the tractor and trailer that make up their rig, and both have been specially modified to the couple's requirements. The tractor is a top-of-the-line 1986 Ford LTL 9000, powered by a Caterpillar diesel engine. The cab has been retrofitted with a sleeper compartment that has two berths and sufficient headroom for the couple to dress standing up—an important consideration when over three hundred days a year are spent on the road. The cab also contains a small refrigerator, camping stove, television, stereo, and sufficient storage for clothing and reading materials. While far from spacious accommodations, the Laffens have certainly outfitted their truck for comfort and efficiency on the road.

As we talked in our hotel room after dinner, David told us how he had become a truck driver after he cashed in his share of the family bicycle store.

I had always wanted to be a truck driver, and after talking with the people in Mayflower's recruiting office I just took them at their word that the business was there and it would be profitable. As a result I held my nose and jumped right off the edge. I went to Sacramento and purchased my truck—I had never even driven one before!

My first tractor cost fifty-six thousand dollars and was two years old when I bought it. A year and a half later I purchased the van, which is unusual—most drivers don't own their own trailers, even after ten years. But I find great satisfaction in owning all my equipment, because that means having it just the way we want it. If you use a company trailer, it's outfitted to haul only one car. We have enough equipment to carry three and quite often we'll move a household and two automobiles. If we had to replace our tractor, trailer, and equipment today, it would cost more than a hundred and sixty thousand dollars.

For four years, David was on the road alone, with the occasional company of a friend from California on a cross-country trip. He was quite content with his life. Looking back, however, he realizes just how difficult those years by himself really were.

Before I met Nancy and was driving alone, there was one couple I especially enjoyed, Larry and Teresa, who don't drive for Mayflower anymore. Every time we were together we enjoyed ourselves. They were a wonderful couple and I always wished I could have something that good, too. And now I do.

Larry would say he couldn't do it without Teresa, and now I understand what he meant. It was very difficult without Nancy. She makes my job a pleasure. Now I have two main jobs that I do—driving, and loading and unloading the trailer. My concentration can be focused on getting there, not on calling people to organize the scheduling of the loading or unloading. Nancy handles that and all the paperwork, in addition to keeping the records and expenses for the accountant.

Nancy does the inventory for every shipment while I'm loading the trailer. It used to take me half a day to do each inventory myself before I could even begin to load the van, and I never finished a job before midnight. Now we're out by seven or eight o'clock without fail. And because she checks over every single item—looking for scratches, loose legs, or other damage before it goes on the truck—our claims rate is very, very low. Most important, she keeps the shipper comfortable and out of my way.

The public relations work she does with our customers is every bit as hard and demanding as the physical work that I do. When we hire a loading crew, she's the one who does the supervision and keeps them hustling because I'm out in the truck orchestrating the loading.

I think men tend to believe that when there's two jobs and one job is moving something—using physical labor—that is more important and harder to do than something that isn't physical. And that's just not true. Nancy's job is every bit as difficult mentally and physically as my job. Lifting things or dealing with people—I can't say one is harder or easier than the other, they're both equally important. The two of us are each doing what we are best at and we're able to do it the way we want to. When you lose your option to do what you want to do, that's what turns a job into work.

Now when drivers talk to us, they're envious when they see us as a couple because we can share our lives together and still earn our living. The married drivers realize just how great it is that we're together, and the single guys see that they don't have to end up alone.

It's a lonely world out there being a truck driver. You're months away from someone you know and years away from someone you might marry. Before I met Nancy, I thought I was getting along just fine—I was very happy with life and with myself. But I'd talked to several husband-and-wife teams and they would say they didn't know how I could do it alone and that it must be hard on me.

David had not expected to meet anyone he would want to marry while he was on the road, because "you're here one day and gone the next. So I had just written off a steady girlfriend or wife until trucking was out of my blood." But after mutual friends introduced them, it didn't take long for David and Nancy to realize that there was something very special between them.

During their six-month courtship, David was requesting shipments to get back to California and they were talking on the telephone every other day. Waiting for loads that would take him home meant lost days and that meant lost money. In spite of Eric's efforts back at the home office to assist the couple, David was able to get home only once or twice a month, and that was certainly not enough time together for either of them. Nancy remembers that when they decided to marry and become a husband-and-wife driving team,

There was really no choice—if we were to be married, then I was going to be on the truck, because David could only get back to California about every two months and sometimes it's only for one or two days. I'd never see him and it wouldn't be worth staying home alone.

In my wildest dreams, I never imagined I'd be a trucker. Before we met, when I was going to college in Sacramento and looking for a job, I thought about applying for a position as a waitress until I found out it was at a truck stop. I said, "No way—I'm not going to work in a *truck stop*." And here I am today—a trucker!

My family was floored when I announced I was marrying a truck driver—it just didn't go over well. But once they met David, they really, really liked him. The entire day of our wedding all I heard was, "If anything happens, it's her fault." I got the distinct feeling that if we got a divorce, they'd adopt him and I'd be out in the cold.

David and Nancy are almost always within arm's reach of each other. While many copreneurial couples are together close to twenty-four hours a day, none of them spends every waking and sleeping moment within touching distance. Most of us would consider working and living together in such a confined space a stressful way to live. However, the Laffens genuinely enjoy their close contact and have learned to deal effectively and on the spot with disagreements, arguments, and stress. When something upsets Nancy, she knows that she can't hold it inside and take a walk around the block—the farthest she can go is into the bunk, just two or three feet away from her husband.

I can't hide my emotions and you can see on my face what's going through my head. At those times, David gives me as much space as he can while he thinks about which one of ten different things might be bothering me—and then I'll tell him it's the eleventh! We talk it out and never really have any big blowouts.

We never go to bed mad at each other. I've tried it and in about two minutes I end up talking through the issue. We discuss our problems with each other and don't try to hide them. We get them out, talk about them, and we understand each other a lot better that way.

Few people realize just how hard the life of a truck driver is. The couple must go weeks and months without a day off, driving their truck and loading and unloading their trailer in all kinds of weather. As David told us,

The weather conditions control you. You're living in the hottest of hot in the summer and the coldest of cold in the winter. You might be in Chicago when it's twenty below with escrow closing the following day. You can't put off moving the customer's belongings just because of the weather. You have to spend twelve hours walking in and out of the house, whether it's freezing cold or blazing hot, loading the van.

And while we've never been late with a delivery, it's not always easy sticking to the schedule. We follow Federal Motor Carrier guidelines—if it's raining, you slow down, if it's snowing or iced, you drive with extreme caution and reduce your speed accordingly.

Moving households entails more than just loading and delivering a cargo. Moves are such stressful occasions that psychologists rank moving as one of the major stresses of life, right up there with the death of a loved one, the loss of a job, or a divorce. Many times when the Laffens arrive at a shipper's home, they can see just how nervous the customers are. To set their minds at ease, David and Nancy go over exactly how they work, what the inventory is for, what they have done in the past—and most important of all, they reassure the customers that their precious possessions are in professional hands. David described the usual reaction.

> Once we've demonstrated that we know what we're doing, our customers bend over backwards for us. They'll go out and get coffee and donuts and pretty soon, they can't do enough. Sometimes they even grab the other end of a couch and help carry it out. And when the time comes for us all to say goodbye, after everything is safely unloaded at the other end, they'll invite us to come back and visit. If we accepted every invitation we get, we'd never get any work done.

The Laffens log more than eighty thousand miles a year, ranking them among the top producers in Mayflower's fleet. Their safety record is outstanding, their damage claims low, and their files simply bulge with letters of commendation from satisfied customers.

When we talked to the people at Mayflower about the Laffens and the other couples who work as independent contractors, there was no doubt from their responses that the company knows the copreneurs in their fleet bring more to the job than just their individual energy and commitment to excellence. Mayflower has learned to recognize when one plus one equals three.

We saved the story of the Laffens and their relationship with Mayflower Transit, Inc. for the last to illustrate that the business community has much to gain from partnerships with entrepreneurial couples. As contractors, franchisees, employees, or commissioned sales representatives, couples working together with the common goal of success for both themselves and the enterprise with which they are affiliated represent a vast untapped potential in the American business community.

In less than a decade, franchising has become big business in the United States, and no discussion of couples working together would be complete without mention of the roles entrepreneurial couples are playing in this expanding segment of the business community. Today there are half a million franchised outlets across the country, and the U.S. Department of Commerce anticipates that sales of goods and services from these businesses will reach almost six hundred and forty billion dollars in 1988—ninety-one percent higher than in 1980 and seven percent higher than 1987.

From businesses as varied as fast food retail outlets, exercise studios, and fully equipped mobile car maintenance vans, the ideas for franchises are boundless. The possibilities are limited only by their founders' abilities to create businesses that satisfy the desire for uniformity, convenience, service, and instant gratification that characterizes today's consumer.

Entrepreneurial couples have played a dual role in the growth of franchising during the 1980s, as both founders and franchise owners. Of the fifty fastest growing new franchises identified by *Venture* magazine for 1988, eleven were founded by copreneurs; and two of the businesses in *Working Together*, T.J. Cinnamons and Christine Valmy, are now the parent companies of nationwide franchise outlets.

Many couples become franchise operators because they feel a need for the guidance and support of the parent company and the ready name recognition that franchises offer. Franchising can present an opportunity to own your own business with the added benefit of an established organization behind you.

The cost of entering into a franchise is as varied as the choice of franchises themselves—a small service company outlet might be obtained for less than ten thousand dollars, while a nationally known fast-food franchise can easily carry a whopping price tag of well over half a million dollars to cover franchise fees, construction, and startup costs. The support offered is just as variable, ranging from a minimal two-day training session to weeks of intensive instruction and on-site consultations.

Franchising may seem attractive, but it should not be viewed as a shortcut to independence. You should invest just as much energy, commitment, and creativity in researching a potential franchise as if you were beginning your venture from the ground up. And once under way, be prepared to work hard; while the organization behind you will lend support, the ultimate success of your venture is up to you.

In this book we have described copreneurs and their individual enterprises and responses to working together. We have illustrated that there are many ways to work together, each as unique as the couples and their businesses. We have shown that couples need not jump head-first into business together, but have the option to test the waters if they choose to do so. Many of the copreneurs in *Working Together* began as coemployees; some founded their ventures with one partner who led the way for the other to join at a later date; and some simply threw caution to the winds, acting on their belief in their enterprise and their ability to succeed.

Working Together will have served its purpose if couples who had not thought about copreneuring are stimulated to consider the possibility; if those who had considered working together now have a better sense of how to go about making their dream a reality; and if entrepreneurial couples already working together have gained a sense of community with others, like themselves, who have put an end to separate lives and separate agendas. And this book will have served its purpose if couples who have no desire to work together have gained insights into their relationships from couples who do.

Finally, this book will have served a broader purpose if it encourages couples to seek employment as a team and if the business community casts aside outdated perceptions and prejudices, accepting couples as team members, while at the same time adopting new styles of management based on freedom from interpersonal competition, open communication, trust, and shared objectives, with couples who work together serving as models.

Our hope for this book, then, is that it will serve as both an inspiration and a challenge—an inspiration to all past, present, and future copreneurs, and a challenge to our society at large to return to traditional values that place the family unit at the heart of the economic system. Today's pioneering copreneurs are leading the way for all of us who wish to gain control of our lives and achieve economic independence.

Appendix

FACTS AT A GLANCE: THE OCCUPATIONS OF THE COPRENEURS IN *WORKING TOGETHER*

Many of the enterprises founded by the copreneurs described in *Working Together* fall into multiple occupational classifications. For example, our advertising agency and writing careers place us under the categories of *Advertising, Authors, Consultants, Direct Mail, Graphic Design*, and *Publishing*. A glance at the following pages will show you just how diverse the activities of the twenty-five businesses included in this book really are. Entrepreneurial couples are innovators and are constantly on the move, fine-tuning their products, services, and enterprises, picking up new skills and expertise along the way.

ADVERTISING

BARNETT/ASSOCIATES, Aptos, California
  Advertising and collateral production agency.
COOKIES FROM HOME, Tempe, Arizona
  Custom corporate promotional cookie gifts.

C & B MOORE PHOTOGRAPHY, Overton, Nevada
  Commercial photography.
RICHARDSON OR RICHARDSON, Phoenix, Arizona
  Advertising agency.
RIVER BANK, INC., Mt. Airy, Maryland
  Political media consultants.

AGRICULTURE
PLANTATION FARM CAMP, INC., Cazadero, California
  Farm and redwood forest management.

ARTISTS
BOB and FRAN HAND, Sag Harbor, New York
  Woodcarvers.
C & B MOORE PHOTOGRAPHY, Overton, Nevada
  Photographers.
DON and AUDREY WOOD, Santa Barbara, California
  Children's book illustrators.

AUCTIONEERS
HARVEY CLAR AUCTION GALLERY, Oakland, California.

AUTHORS
BARNETT/ASSOCIATES, Aptos, California
  Technical and advertising copy writers and nonfiction
  authors.
GEORGE GERMON and JOHANNE KILLEEN, Providence,
Rhode Island
  Cookbook authors.
RUTH McCLENDON and LESLIE KADIS, Aptos, California
  Nonfiction authors.
JOE ORTIZ, Capitola, California
  Cookbook author.
DON and AUDREY WOOD, Santa Barbara, California
  Children's book authors.

CATERING
GAYLE'S BAKERY AND ROSTICCERIA,
Capitola, California.

CONSULTANTS
BARNETT/ASSOCIATES, Aptos, California
  Marketing.

HARVEY CLAR AUCTION GALLERY, Oakland, California
   Appraisals.
THE INSTITUTE FOR FAMILY BUSINESS,
Aptos, California
   Mental health and family firm therapy.
RICHARDSON OR RICHARDSON, Phoenix, Arizona
   Marketing and golf course design.
RIVER BANK, INC., Mt. Airy, Maryland
   Political media consultants.

DIRECT MAIL

BARNETT/ASSOCIATES, Aptos, California
   Production of direct mail promotion incentives.
COOKIES FROM HOME, Tempe, Arizona
   Direct mail marketing and sales.
THE RENOVATOR'S SUPPLY, Millers Falls, Massachusetts
   Catalog sales.
RICHARDSON OR RICHARDSON, Phoenix, Arizona
   Production of direct mail promotions.

ENTERTAINERS

PAM and RANDY DOUGHERTY, Phoenix, Arizona
   Square-dance callers.

FASHION

SAM & LIBBY, CALIFORNIA, San Carlos, California
   Women's fashion shoe designers and manufacturers.

FRANCHISERS

CHRISTINE VALMY, INC., Pine Brook, New Jersey
   Skin care salons.
T.J. CINNAMONS, Kansas City, Missouri
   T.J. Cinnamons Bakeries.

GRAPHIC DESIGNERS

BARNETT/ASSOCIATES, Aptos, California.
RICHARDSON OR RICHARDSON, Phoenix, Arizona.

HEALTH CARE PROVIDERS

HANDLOFF CHIROPRACTIC, Santa Cruz, California
   Chiropractic, acupuncture, and shiatsu therapy.

THE INSTITUTE FOR FAMILY BUSINESS,
Aptos, California
   Family business and individual therapy.
KINGS ROAD PET HOSPITAL, Reno, Nevada
   Veterinary clinic.

LEISURE SERVICES

PAM and RANDY DOUGHERTY, Phoenix, Arizona
   Square dance callers.
GOLD CANYON STABLES, Apache Junction, Arizona
   Riding stables and pack trips.
PLANTATION FARM CAMP, INC., Cazadero, California
   Working farm children's summer camp.

MANUFACTURING

CHALIF INC., Wyndmoor, Pennsylvania
   Gourmet mustards and condiments.
CHRISTINE VALMY, INC., Pine Brook, New Jersey
   Skin care products.
COOKIES FROM HOME, Tempe, Arizona
   Ready to bake cookies.
HARPER HOUSE, INC., Culver City, California
   Day Runner personal management organizers.
THE RENOVATOR'S SUPPLY, Millers Falls, Massachusetts
   Home restoration products.
SAM & LIBBY, CALIFORNIA, San Carlos, California
   Women's fashion shoes.

PERSONNEL SERVICES

IRENE COHEN PERSONNEL SERVICES,
New York, New York
   Personnel placement and employee leasing services.

PHOTOGRAPHY

C & B MOORE PHOTOGRAPHY, Overton, Nevada
   Nature and rodeo photography.
RIVER BANK, INC., Mt. Airy, Maryland
   Political television commercials.

PUBLISHING

BARNETT/ASSOCIATES, Aptos, California
  Collateral publications, book production and nonfiction
  authors.

GEORGE GERMON and JOHANNE KILLEEN, Providence,
Rhode Island
  Cookbook authors.

HARPER HOUSE, INC., Culver City, California
  Day Runner personal management organizers.

RUTH McCLENDON and LESLIE KADIS, Aptos, California
  Nonfiction authors.

JOE ORTIZ, Capitola, California
  Cookbook author.

THE RENOVATOR'S SUPPLY, Millers Falls, Massachusetts
  Catalogs and *Victorian Homes* magazine.

DON and AUDREY WOOD, Santa Barbara, California
  Children's book authors and illustrators.

RESTAURANTS, DELICATESSENS, AND NIGHT CLUBS

AL FORNO, Providence, Rhode Island.

GAYLE'S ROSTICCERIA, Capitola, California.

THE HOT CLUB, Providence, Rhode Island.

LUCKY'S, Providence, Rhode Island.

RETAIL

CHRISTINE VALMY, INC., Pine Brook, New Jersey
  National and international franchise outlets.

COOKIES FROM HOME, Tempe, Arizona
  Retail store.

GAYLE'S BAKERY AND ROSTICCERIA, Capitola, California
  French bakery and delicatessen.

RAKESTRAW BOOKS, Danville, California
  Bookstore.

T.J. CINNAMONS BAKERY, Kansas City, Missouri
  National franchise bakery outlets.

THERAPISTS

THE INSTITUTE FOR FAMILY BUSINESS,
Aptos, California
  Family business and individual therapy.

TRUCKING

MAYFLOWER TRANSIT, INC., Indianapolis, Indiana
  David and Nancy Laffen, owner/operators, Novato,
  California.

VIDEO PRODUCTION

RIVER BANK, INC., Mt. Airy, Maryland
  Political television commercials.

VOCATIONAL SCHOOLS

CHRISTINE VALMY, INC., Pine Brook, New Jersey
  National and international skin care schools.
IRENE COHEN PERSONNEL SERVICES,
New York, New York
  Word processing and computer training center.

THE TWENTY-FIVE COUPLES WHOSE
STORIES APPEAR IN *WORKING TOGETHER*

Frank and Sharan Barnett
BARNETT/ASSOCIATES
Aptos, California

Barry and Susan Brooks
COOKIES FROM HOME
Tempe, Arizona

David and Suzanne Brown
PLANTATION FARM CAMP, INC.
Cazadero, California

Harvey and Donna Clar
HARVEY CLAR AUCTION GALLERY
Oakland, California

Sy and Irene Cohen
IRENE COHEN PERSONNEL SERVICES
New York, New York

Peter and Marina de Haydu
CHRISTINE VALMY, INC.
Pine Brook, New Jersey

Don and Shelley Donnelly
GOLD CANYON STABLES
Apache Junction, Arizona

Tom and Sharon Dose
KINGS ROAD PET HOSPITAL
Reno, Nevada

Randy and Pam Dougherty
Square Dance Callers
Phoenix, Arizona

Sam and Libby Edelman
  SAM & LIBBY, CALIFORNIA
  San Carlos, California

George Germon and Johanne Killeen
  LUCKY'S
  AL FORNO
  THE HOT CLUB
  Providence, Rhode Island

Bob and Fran Hand
  Woodcarvers
  Sag Harbor, New York

Bruce and Masami Handloff
  HANDLOFF CHIROPRACTIC
  Santa Cruz, California

Brian and Mary Harvey
  RAKESTRAW BOOKS
  Danville, California

Claude and Donna Jeanloz
  THE RENOVATOR'S SUPPLY, INC.
  Millers Falls, Massachusetts

Leslie Kadis and Ruth McClendon
  THE INSTITUTE FOR FAMILY BUSINESS
  Aptos, California

David and Nancy Laffen
  Novato, California
  Owner/Operators for
  MAYFLOWER TRANSIT, INC.
  Indianapolis, Indiana

Clif and Beth Moore
  C & B MOORE PHOTOGRAPHY
  Overton, Nevada

Joe and Gayle Ortiz
GAYLE'S BAKERY AND ROSTICCERIA
Capitola, California

Ted and Joyce Rice
T.J. CINNAMONS
Kansas City, Missouri

Forrest and Valerie Richardson
RICHARDSON OR RICHARDSON
Phoenix, Arizona

Nick and Liz Thomas
CHALIF INC.
Wyndmoor, Pennsylvania

Ian and Betsy Weinschel
RIVER BANK, INC.
Mt. Airy, Maryland

Boyd and Felice Willat
HARPER HOUSE, INC.
Culver City, California

Don and Audrey Wood
Children's Book Authors and Illustrators
Santa Barbara, California

Index

expectations, 99
traditional, 98–100
sharing, 64, 65–69, 73–76
Roles and tasks
    See Working styles
Romance
    in the office, xxii–xxiii
    in copreneuring, xxiii, 97
Roper poll, xxvi

S

Sam & Libby, California, 16, 18,
    19, 57, 110, 142, 143, 181, 191
    See also Edelman, Sam and
        Libby
Sax, Richard, 39
Self-made couple, 11
Self-reliance, 4, 9
Seventeen, 17
Signature Foods, Inc., 137
    See also Rice, Ted and Joyce
Small Business Administration,
    xxvi, xxvii
Small businesses
    growth of, xxvii–xxviii
    job security, xxvii
Social life, 191–94, 198
Sole proprietorship, 121–22
Square dance callers, 178–79
    See also Dougherty, Randy and
        Pam
Strengths, maximizing individual,
    26, 59–60, 91, 133–34
Success, elements for, 101–05
Sweat equity, 108, 186
Synergism, 5, 59–60, 72, 204

T

T.J. Cinnamons, 36, 37, 57, 137,
    138, 140, 187, 213
    See also Rice, Ted and Joyce
Takigawa & Co., Ltd., 90
Talents, maximizing individual,
    59–60
Tax Reform Act of 1986, 123
Teamwork, 30, 55, 59–60, 81, 82,
    103–05, 133, 139, 143, 146, 210,
    214–15

Technology, appropriate, xxvi, 64,
    116–20
Testing the waters, 15–19, 133, 214
Therapy, 163–64, 180
Think tank, the three hundred
    percent, 59–60
Thomas, Nick and Liz, 31–33, 49,
    108–10, 135–37, 140, 180, 187–88
    See also Chalif Inc.; Hill, Joe
Time for yourself, 179–82
Time off and time out, 191–97
Trucking, husband and wife driving
    teams, 177, 205–12
    See also Laffen, David and
        Nancy
Trucking industry, deregulation,
    205, 206
    See also Mayflower Transit, Inc.
Trust, xxv, 3, 10, 91, 101, 103–04,
    137, 141, 159, 168, 214

U

Undercapitalization, 26, 108
U.S. Bureau of Labor Statistics, xxvii
U.S. Department of Commerce, 213

V

Vacations, 194–97
Valmy, Christine, 86–87, 89, 91
    See also Christine Valmy, Inc.;
        de Haydu, Peter and Marina
Venture capital, 58–59, 204
Venture, 36, 231
Victorian Homes, 84, 85
    See also Jeanloz, Claude and
        Donna
Voluntary simplicity, 69, 177–79,
    182

W

Weaknesses, minimizing individual,
    59–60, 133
Wego, 9, 93–95, 100, 101, 105, 140
    See also egos
Weinschel, Ian and Betsy, 19–21,
    144, 194–95
    See also River Bank, Inc.

COPRENEURS™
The Newsletter for Entrepreneurial Couples.

As cofounders of the National Association of Entrepreneurial Couples, Frank and Sharan Barnett invite you to subscribe to COPRENEURS,™ a quarterly newsletter devoted to topics of interest to every couple who have made the decision to work together and regain positive control of their lives.

COPRENEURS focuses on today's economic pioneers who are building a new kind of partnership based on trust, equality, sharing, and intimacy between partners. Your subscription will bring you informative, entertaining, and provocative news about a new way of living that incorporates the work and personal worlds into a harmonious whole.

To receive COPRENEURS, fill out the form below and send it to us along with your check or money order for $15, payable to the National Association of Entrepreneurial Couples. Your one-year subscription will begin with the next issue.

MAIL TO:
COPRENEURS
NAEC
P.O. Box 825
Belmont, CA 94002

Please enter my one-year subscription to COPRENEURS,™ a quarterly publication. My payment of $15 is enclosed, payable to the National Association of Entrepreneurial Couples.

Name_____

Company_____

Address_____

City_____State_____Zip_____

COPRENEURS—the newsletter for every couple who wish to put an end to separate lives and separate agendas.

About the Authors

Coentrepreneurs in their own advertising agency, Frank and Sharan Barnett come to their role as observers of contemporary American culture from diverse backgrounds. Sharan has been a broadcast journalist, and for eight years worked in the field of juvenile corrections. Frank, a lifelong entrepreneur, received his undergraduate and graduate degrees in anthropology from the University of California at Berkeley and at Los Angeles. The couple are cofounders of the National Association of Entrepreneurial Couples, located in Belmont, California, and publish *Copreneurs: The Newsletter For Entrepreneurial Couples*. The Barnetts and their three children, Anthony, Elliott and Kimberly, make their home in Aptos, California.